HACKIN

The Ultimate Guide for Y
Hidden secrets of Hacking

I0004689

By Emily Goldstein

Table of Contents

INTRODUCTION

I assume there are a few inquiries that may be going through your mind as you consider perusing this book: Who is the target group for this book? How this book is not quite the same as book "x" (embed your most loved title here)?

Why would it be a good idea for me to purchase it? Since these are every reasonable inquiry and I am asking you to plunk down your well-deserved money, it is imperative to give a few answers to these inquiries.

For individuals who are occupied with finding out about hacking and entrance testing, strolling into a very much loaded book shop can be as confounding as looking for "hacking" books at amazon.com. At first, there seems, by all accounts, to be a just about unending determination to browse. Most vast book shops have a few racks committed to PC security books. They incorporate books on programming security, web application security, rootkits and malware, entrance testing, what's more, obviously, hacking. On the other hand, even the hacking books appear to shift in substance what's more, topic. A few books concentrate on utilizing instruments however don't examine how these instruments fit together. Different books concentrate on hacking a specific subject yet, do not have the expansive picture. This book is expected to address these issues. It is intended to be a solitary beginning point for anybody keen on the points of hacking or entrance testing. The book will surely cover particular instruments and themes yet will likewise analyze how the apparatuses fit together and how they depend on each other to be effective.

WHO IS THE INTENDED AUDIENCE FOR THIS BOOK?

This book is intended to be an exceptionally delicate yet exhaustive manual for the universe of hack- ing and infiltration testing. it is particularly gone for helping you ace the essential steps expected to finish a hack or entrance test without overpowering you. When you complete this book, you will have a strong comprehension of the infiltration testing procedure and you will be OK with the essential devices expected to finish the occupation.

in particular, this book is gone for individuals who are new to the universe of hack- ing and entrance testing, for those with practically zero past experience, for the individuals who are baffled by the failure to see the master plan (how the different instruments and stages fit together), or for those hoping to extend their insight into hostile security.

In short, this book is composed for any individual who is occupied with PC security, hacking, or entrance testing but has no related knowledge and is not certain where to start. An associate and I call this idea "zero passage hacking" (ZeH), much like current swimming pools. Zero passage pools steadily incline from the dry end to the profound end, permitting swimmers to wade in without feeling overpowered or without having an apprehension of suffocating. The "zero passage" idea permits everybody the capacity to utilize the pool paying little heed to age or swimming ability. This book utilizes a comparable system. ZeH is intended to open you to the essential ideas without overpowering you. Consummation of ZeH will set you up for cutting edge courses and books.

HOW IS THIS BOOK DIFFERENT FROM BOOK 'X'?

Winnow investing energy with my family, there are two things I appreciate doing: perusing and hacking. More often than not, I consolidate these diversions by perusing about hacking. As an educator and an infiltration analyzer, you can envision that my bookshelf is lined with numerous books on hacking, security, and entrance testing. Likewise with most things in life, the quality and estimation of each book is diverse. a few books are astounding assets that have been utilized such a variety of times that the ties are truly going into disrepair. Others are less useful and stay in about new condition. A book that benefits an occupation of clarifying the subtle elements without losing the per user is justified, despite all the trouble's weight in gold. Sadly, the majority of my personal top picks, those that are worn and battered, are either exceptionally extensive (500 ☐ pages) or extremely centered (an inside and out manual for a solitary subject). Neither of these is a terrible thing; truth be told, an incredible inverse, it is the level of point of interest and the clarity of the creators' clarification that make them so extraordinary. Yet, in the meantime, a substantial tome concentrated on a natty gritty subject of security can appear to be overpowering to newcomers.

Tragically, as an amateur attempting to break into the security field and take in the nuts and bolts of hacking, handling one of these books can be both overwhelming and confounding. This book is not the same as different distributions in two ways. to start with, it is implied for novices; review the idea of "zero passage." on the off chance that you have never per- shaped any kind of hacking or you have utilized a couple instruments yet are not exactly beyond any doubt what to do next (or how to translate the consequences of the apparatus), this book is for you. The objective is not to cover you with points of interest but rather to present an expansive outline of the whole field.

Normally, the book will even now cover each of the significant devices expected to finish the progressions in an infiltration test, yet it won't stop to analyze the entire top to bottom or extra usefulness for each of these instruments. This will be useful from the outlook that it will concentrate on the fundamentals and much of the time permit us to evade disarray brought about by cutting edge elements or minor contrasts in device renditions.

For instance, when we examine port filtering, the section will talk about how to run the essential sweeps with the exceptionally well known port scanner nmap. Since the book concentrates on the nuts and bolts, it turns out to be less critical precisely which form of nmap the client is running. Running a sYn output utilizing nmap is precisely the same respect less of whether you are directing your sweep with nmap adaptation 2 or rendition 5. this system will be utilized as regularly as could be allowed, doing as such ought to permit the peruser to learn nmap (or any apparatus) without needing to stress over the adjustments in usefulness that regularly go hand in hand with cutting edge includes in adaptation changes. The objective of this book is to give general learning that will permit you to handle propelled subjects and books. Keep in mind, once you have a firm handle of the fundamentals, you can simply do a reversal and take in the particular points of interest and propelled elements of an instrument. Furthermore, every part will end with a rundown of proposed devices and points that are outside the extent of this book yet can be utilized for hide ther study and to propel your insight.

Past simply being composed for learners, this book really introduces the information in an exceptionally remarkable manner. All the instruments and procedures we use in this book will be completed in a particular request against a little number of related focuses on (all objective machines will fit in with the same subnet, and the peruser will have the capacity to effortlessly reproduce this "objective" system to take after along). Perusers will be demonstrated to decipher instrument yield and how to use that yield to proceed with the assault starting with one part then onto the next. The utilization of a consecutive and solitary moving illustration all through the book will help perusers see the master plan and better fathom how the different instruments and stages fit together. This is not quite the same as numerous different books on the scratch ket today, which frequently examine different devices and assaults yet neglect to clarify how those apparatuses can be successfully fastened together. Displaying data in a manner that demonstrates to the client industry standards to plainly move starting with one stage then onto the next will give profitable experience and permit the peruser to finish a whole penetration test by basically taking after alongside the cases in the book. This concept ought to permit the peruser to get a reasonable comprehension of the major information while figuring out how the different apparatuses and stages interface

CHAPTER 1: AN OVERVIEW OF HACKING AND PENETRATION TESTING

Penetration testing can be characterized as a lawful and approved endeavor to find and effectively misuse PC frameworks with the end goal of making those systems more secure. the procedure incorporates testing for vulnerabilities and in addition giving evidence of idea (Poc) assaults to exhibit the vulnerabilities are genuine. Fitting penetration testing dependably closes with particular proposals for tending to and settling the issues that were found amid the test. Overall, this procedure is utilized to help secure PCs and systems against future assaults.

Penetration testing is otherwise called:

- nenP
- n Pt
- testing
- n Hacking
- n ethical Hacking
- n white Hat Hacking

It is vital to spend a couple of minutes talking about the distinction between penetration testing and weakness evaluation. Numerous individuals (and sellers) in the security group inaccurately utilize these terms reciprocally. A vulnercapacity evaluation is the procedure of checking on administrations and frameworks for potential security issues, though a penetration test really performs abuse and Poc assaults to demonstrate that a security issue exists. Penetration tests go a stage past defenselessness evaluations by reenacting programmer movement and conveying live payloads. In this book, we will cover the procedure of helplessness evaluation as one of the strides used to finish a penetration test.

Setting the Stage

Seeing all the different players and positions in the realm of hacking and penetration testing is integral to grasping the broad view. Give us a chance to begin by painting the photo with wide brush strokes. Kindly comprehend that the accompanying is a gross misrepresentation; be that as it may, it ought to help you see the differences between the different gatherings of individuals included.

It may help to consider the Star Wars universe where there are two sides of the "power": Jedis and siths. Great versus fiendish, both sides have entry to a unimaginable force. One side uses its energy to secure and serve, while the other side uses it for individual addition and misuse.

Figuring out how to hack is much like figuring out how to utilize the power (or somewhere in the vicinity I envision!). The more you take in, the more power you have. in the long run, you will need to choose whether you will utilize your energy for good or awful. There is an excellent publication from the Star Wars scene in motion picture that portrays Anakin as a young man. On the off chance that you take a gander at Anakin's shadow in the blurb, you will see it is the blueprint of darth Vader. Take a stab at looking the web for "Anakin darth Vader shadow" to see it. Understanding why this publication has bid is discriminating. As a kid, Anakin had no desires of getting to be darth Vader, yet it happened regardless.

It is most likely safe to expect that not very many individuals get into hacking to turn into a super scalawag. The issue is that voyage to the dark side is a tricky slant. On the other hand, on the off chance that you need to be incredible, have the admiration of your associates, and be pick up completely utilized in the security workforce, you have to confer yourself to utilizing your forces to secure and serve. Having a crime on your record is a restricted ticket to another calling. Doubtlessly there is at present a deficiency of qualified security specialists, yet even along these lines, relatively few bosses today are willing to take a risk, particularly if those unlawful acts include PCs. in the pen testing world, it is not remarkable to hear the expressions "white hat" and "black hat" to portray the Jedis and siths. all through this book, the expressions "white hat," "ethical programmer," or "penetration analyzer" will be utilized exchange capably to portray the Jedis. the siths will be alluded to as "black hats," "breakers," or "malignant attackers." it is imperative to note that ethical programmers complete large portions of the same activities with a number of the same instruments as malevolent attackers. in about every situation, an ethical programmer ought to endeavor to act and take on a similar mindset as a genuine black hat programmer. The closer the penetration test reenacts a genuine assault, the more esteem it gives to the client paying to the Pt.

If it's not too much trouble take note of how the past section says "in almost every circumstance." despite the fact that white hats complete a significant number of the same errands with a considerable lot of the same instruments, there is a huge improvement between the two sides. At its center, these contrasts can be come down to three key focuses: approval, inspiration, and plan. it ought to be focused on that these focuses are not comprehensive, but rather they can be valuable in figuring out whether a movement is ethical or not. The primary and easiest approach to separate between white hats and black hats is approval. Approval is the procedure of getting endorsement before con- ducting any tests or assaults. When approval is acquired, both the penetration analyzer and the organization being evaluated need to concur upon the extent of the test. The extension incorporates particular data about the assets and frameworks to be incorporated in the test. The extension unequivocally characterizes the approved focuses for the penetration analyzer. It is imperative that both sides completely comprehend the approval and extent of the Pt. White hats should dependably regard the authorization and stay inside of the extent of the test. Black hats will have no such requirements on the objective rundown.

The second approach to separate between an ethical programmer and a malignant programmer is through examination of the attacker's inspiration. on the off chance that the attacker is propelled or driven by individual addition, including benefit through blackmail or different shrewd techniques for gathering cash from the casualty, requital, acclaim, or the like, he or she ought to be viewed as a black hat. Then again, if the attacker is preauthorized and his or her inspiration is to help the association and enhance their security, he or she can be viewed as a white hat. At long last, if the goal is to give the association a sensible assault simulation so that the organization can enhance its security through ahead of schedule disclosure and moderation of vulnerabilities, the attacker ought to be viewed as a white hat. It is additionally imperative to grasp the basic way of keeping Pt discoveries secret. Ethical programmers will never share touchy data found amid the procedure of a penetration testing with anybody other than the customer. Notwithstanding, if the aim is to influence data for individual benefit or addition, the attacker ought to be viewed as a black hat.

Introduction With BACKTRACK LINUX: Bunches of TOOLS

A couple of years back, the open talk or instructing of hacking methods was viewed as somewhat unthinkable. Luckily, things are different now and individuals are starting to comprehend the estimation of hostile security. Hostile security is currently being grasped by associations paying little heed to size or commercial ventures. Governments are likewise quitting any and all funny business about hostile security. Numerous administrations have gone on record expressing they are effectively building and creating hostile security capacities.

Eventually, penetration testing ought to assume an imperative part in the general security of your association. Pretty much as approaches, danger appraisals, business continuity arranging, and debacle recuperation have get to be necessary parts in keeping your association sheltered and secure, penetration testing should be incorporated in your general security arrange also. Penetration testing permits you to view your association through the eyes of the adversary. This procedure can prompt numerous astounding revelations and give you the time expected to fix your systems before a genuine attacker can strike. An extraordinary aspect regarding figuring out how to hack today is the plenty and accessibility of good apparatuses to perform your specialty. Not just are the apparatuses readily accessible, however a significant number of them are stable with quite a while of improvement behind them. Perhaps more critical to a significant number of you is the way that the majority of these instruments are accessible gratis. With the end goal of this book, each apparatus secured will be free. It is one thing to know an apparatus is free; it is another to discover, arrange, and introduce each of the devices needed to finish even an essential penetration test. In spite of the fact that this procedure is very straightforward on today's present day Linux, it can even now be somewhat overwhelming for newcomers. A great many people who begin are generally more inspired by figuring out how to utilize the apparatuses than they are in looking the immeasurable corners of the web finding and introducing instruments. To be reasonable, you truly ought to figure out how to physically assemble and introduce delicate product on a Linux machine; or at any rate, you ought to end up acquainted with able get (or the like).

A fundamental comprehension of Linux will be gainful and will pay you heaps of profits over the long haul. With the end goal of this book, there will be no presumption that you have former Linux experience, however help yourself out and submit yourself to turning into a Linux master sometime in the not so distant future. Take a class, read a book, or simply investigate all alone. Trust me; you will say thanks to me later. In the event that you are between interested in penetration testing or hacking, there is no chance to get of getting around the need to know Linux. Luckily, the security group is an exceptionally dynamic and extremely giving gathering. There are a few associations that have worked energetically to make different security-particular Linux conveyances. A dispersion, or "distro" for short, is basically a flavor, sort, or brand of Linux.

Among the most no doubt understood of these penetration testing dispersions is one called "Backtrack." Backtrack Linux is your one-stop search for learning hacking and performing penetration testing. Backtrack Linux helps me to remember that scene in the first Matrix motion picture where tank asks neo "what do you require other than a supernatural occurrence?" neo reacts with "weapons, bunches of firearms." At this point in the motion picture, columns and lines of weapons slide into perspective. Each weapon possible is accessible for neo and trinity: handguns, rifles, shotguns, self-loader, programmed, of all shapes and sizes from guns to explosives, a perpetual supply of diverse weapons from which to pick. That is a comparative affair most newcomers have when they first boot up Backtrack. "devices. heaps of devices."

Backtrack Linux is a programmer's blessing from heaven. the whole appropriation is developed from the beginning penetration analyzers. the appropriation comes preloaded with many security apparatuses that are introduced, arranged, and prepared to be utilized. Best of all, Backtrack is free! You can get your duplicate at http://www. Backtrack-linux.org/downloads/. exploring to the Backtrack connection will permit you to browse either an .iso or a Vmware picture. on the off chance that you decide to download the .iso, you will need to smolder the .iso to a dVd. on the off chance that you are uncertain of how to finish this procedure, please Google "copying an iso." Once you have finished the copying procedure, you will have a bootable

DVD. Much of the time, beginning Backtrack from a bootable dVd is as straightforward as putting the dVd into the drive and restarting the machine. In a few occurrences, you may need to change the boot arrange in the Bios so that the optical drive has the most astounding boot need. On the off chance that you decide to download the Vmware picture, you will likewise require programming fit for opening and conveying or running the picture.

Fortunately enough, there are a few decent devices for fulfilling this assignment. contingent upon your lean toward ence, you can utilize'sVmware Player, sun microsystem's VirtualBox, or microsoft's Virtual Pc. In all actuality, in the event that you don't care for any of those choices, there are numerous other programming alternatives fit for running a Vm picture. You essentially need to pick one that you are alright with. each of the three virtualization alternatives recorded above are accessible for nothing out of pocket and will give you the capacity to run Vm pictures. You will need todecide which version is best for you. this book will rely heavily on the use of a Backtrack Vmware image and Vmware Player. At the time of writing, Vmware Player was available at: http://www.vmware.com/products/player/. You will need to register for an account to download the software, but the registration process is simple and free.

If you are unsure of which option to choose, it is suggested that you go the Vmware route. not only is this another good technology to learn, but using Vms will allow you to set up an entire penetration testing lab on a single machine. If that machine is a laptop, you essentially have a "travelling" Pt lab so you can practice your skills anytime, anywhere.

If you choose to run Backtrack using the bootable DVD, shortly after the sys- tem starts, you will be presented with a menu list. You will need to review the list carefully, as it contains several different options. The first couple of options are used to set some basic information about your system's screen resolution. If you are having trouble getting Backtrack to boot, be sure to choose the "start Backtrack in safe graphical mode." The menu contains several other options, but these are outside the scope of this book. to select the desired boot option, simply use the arrow keys to highlight the appropriate row and hit the enter key to confirm your selection.

The use of Backtrack is not required to work through this book or to learn the basics of hacking. Any version of Linux will do fine. the major advantage of using Backtrack is that all the tools are preloaded for you. If you choose to use a different version of Linux, you will need to install the tools before reading the chapter. It is also important to remember that because this book focuses on the basics, it does not matter which version of Backtrack you are using. All the tools we will explore and use in this book are available in every version.

WORKING WITH BACKTRACK:
STARTING THE ENGINE

Regardless of whether you choose to run Backtrack as a Vm or boot to a live dVd, once the initial system is loaded you will be presented with a log-in prompt. the default username is root and the default password is toor.notice the default secret word is basically "root" spelled in reverse. this default username and watchword blend has been being used subsequent to Backtrack 1, and no doubt it will stay being used for future forms. Right now, you ought to be signed into the framework and ought to be given "root@bt:~#" brief. Despite the fact that it is conceivable to run large portions of the instruments we will talk about in this book straightforwardly from the terminal, it is frequently simpler for newcomers to make utilization of the x window framework. You can begin the gUi by writing the accompanying command after the "root@bt~#" brief:

Startx

Subsequent to writing this summon and hitting the enter key, x will start to load. this environment ought to appear to be ambiguously natural to most PC clients. when it has totally stacked, you will see a desktop, symbols, an errand bar, and a framework plate. Much the same as Microsoft windows, you can associate with these things by moving your mouse cursor and tapping on the sought article. the majority of the projects we will use in this book will be come up short on the terminal. You can begin a terminal session by either tapping on the black box situated in the lower left in the taskbar, or by writing the accompanying order into the launcher.

Konsole

Dissimilar to Microsoft windows or a number of the advanced linuxos's, of course, Backtrack does not accompany systems administration empowered. this setup is by configuration. As a penetration analyzer, we frequently attempt to keep up a stealthy or undetected pres- ence. nothing shouts "take a gander At me!! take a gander At me!! I'm Here!!!" like a PC that begins up and in a split second starts retching system movement by expansive throwing solicitations for a dHcP server and IP address. To dodge this issue, the net- working interfaces of your Backtrack machine are turned down (off) naturally. The least demanding approach to empower systems administration is through the terminal. Open a terminal window by tapping on the terminal symbol. Once the terminal opens, enter the accompanying summon:

Ifconfig –a

This summon will list all the accessible interfaces for your machine. At any rate, most machines will incorporate an eth0 and a lo interface. The "lo" interface is your loopback interface. the "eth0" is your first Ethernet card. Contingent

31

upon your equipment, you may have extra interfaces or vary ent interface numbers recorded. On the off chance that you are running Backtrack through a Vm, your principle interface will typically be eth0. To turn the system card on, you enter the accompanying order into a terminal window:

Ifconfig eth0 up

Give us a chance to inspect this charge in more detail; "ifconfig" is a Linux order that signifies "I need to design a system interface." As we probably am aware, "eth0" is the first system gadget on our framework (recall PCs regularly begin tallying at 0 not 1), and the magic word "up" is utilized to initiate the between face. so we can generally interpret the summon you entered as "I need to con- figure the first interface to be turned on." Since the interface is turned on, we have to get an iP address. there are two fundamental approaches to finish this assignment. Our first alternative is to relegate the location physically by affixing the craved iP location to the end of the past command. case in point, in the event that we needed to relegate our system card an IP location of 192.168.1.23, we would sort:

ifconfig eth0 up 192.168.1.23

Right now, the machine will have an iP address yet will at present need an entryway and space name framework (dns) server. A straightforward google hunt down "setting up niclinux" will demonstrate to you industry standards to enter that data. You can simply verify whether your summons worked by issuing the accompanying summon into a terminal window:

ifconfig

rthuinsnwinilgl permit you to see the present settings for your system between faces. Since this is an apprentice's aide and for the purpose of straightforwardness, we will accept that stealth is not a worry right now. all things considered, the most straightforward approach to get a location is to utilize dHcP. to allocate a location through dHcP, you basically issue the summon:

dhclient eth0

It would be ideal if you take note of, this accept you have as of now effectively run the order to turn up your system interface (eth0 for this situation). since we have effectively doled out an iP address, the exact opposite thing to deliver is the means by which to kill Backtrack. Likewise with most things in Linux, there are various approaches to perform this undertaking. one of the most effortless courses is to enter the accompanying order into a terminal window:

poweroff

You can likewise substitute the poweroff order with the reboot charge on the off chance that you would like to restart the framework as opposed to close it down.

Before continuing, you ought to take a few minutes to survey and practice all the strides highlighted so far including

nowPer on/ start up Backtrack

n sign in with the default client name and watchword

n begin x (the windows gUi)

n View all the system interfaces on your machine

n turn up (on) the wanted system interface

n Assign an iP address physically

n View the physically doled out iP address

n Assign an iP address through dHcP

n View the alterably allocated location

n reboot the machine utilizing the charge line interface

nowPeroff the machine utilizing the charge line interface

THE USE AND CREATION OF A HACKING LAB

Every ethical programmer must have a spot to practice and investigate. most newcomers are befuddled about how they can figure out how to utilize hacking devices without violating the law or assaulting unapproved targets. this is frequently fulfilled through the production of an individual "hacking lab." A hacking lab is a sandboxed environment where your movement and assaults have no possibility of getting away or coming to unauthorized and unintended targets. in this environment, you are allowed to investigate all the different instruments and strategies without trepidation that some movement or assault will get away from your system.

At any rate, the lab is situated up to contain no less than two machines: one attacker and one casualty. in different arrangements, a few casualty machines can be conveyed at the same time to recreate a more practical system. the best possible utilization and setup of a hacking lab is indispensable on the grounds that a standout amongst the best intends to learn something is by doing that thing. learning and experting the nuts and bolts of penetration testing is the same. the absolute most critical purpose of any programmer lab is the segregation of the system.

You must arrange your lab organize in such a path, to the point that it is unthinkable for movement to escape or go outside of the system. oversights happen and even the most watchful individuals can fat-finger or mistype an iP address. it is a straightforward mix-up to mistype a solitary digit in an iP address, however that confuse can have radical results for you and your future. it would be a disgrace (and all the more vitally illicit) for you to run a progression of outputs and assaults against what you believed was your programmer lab focus with an iP location of 172.16.1.1 just to figure out later that you really entered the iP address as 122.16.1.1.

The least complex and best approach to make a sandboxed or secluded environment is to physically unplug or separate your system from the web. in the event that you are utilizing physical machines, it is best to depend on hardwired Ethernet links and changes to course activity. Additionally make sure to twofold and triple-watch that the majority of your remote nics are killed. Continuously deliberately review and audit your net- work for potential holes before proceeding

CHAPTER 2: DIFFERENT TYPES OF HACKERS AND THEIR VARIOUS SKILL LEVELS

Programmer" is a free term and has diverse implications. By and large the expression "Programmer" is somebody who breaks into PC systems for the joy he gets from the test of doing it or with some different expectations like taking information for cash or with political inspirations. Programmers are ordered to distinctive sorts. Some of them are recorded beneath.

White Hat: A White Hat programmer is a PC system security proficient and has non-malevolent goal at whatever point he breaks into security frameworks. A White Hat programmer has profound information in Computer Networking, Network Protocols and System Administration (no less than three or four Operating Systems and great abilities in

Scripting and Programming). White Hat programmer has additionally great information in hacking devices and knows how to program hacking apparatuses.

A White Hat programmer has what it takes to break into systems however he utilizes his aptitudes to ensure associations. A White Hat programmer can lead powerlessness evaluations and penetration tests are otherwise called an Ethical Hacker. Frequently White Hat programmers are utilized by organizations and associations to check the vulnerabilities of their system and verify that no gap is accessible in their system for an interloper.

Black Hat: A Black Hat programmer, otherwise called a saltine, is a PC proficient with profound information in Computer Networking, Network Protocols and System Administration (no less than three or four Operating Systems and great abilities in Scripting and Programming). Black Hat programmer has additionally great information in numerous hacking devices and knows how to program hacking instruments. A Black Hat programmer uses his abilities for unethical reasons. A Black Hat programmer dependably has malignant goal for interrupting a system. Sample: To take research information from an organization, To take cash from Visas, Hack Email Accounts and so on.

Dim Hat: A Gray Hat programmer is somebody who is between White Hat programmer and Black Hat programmer. Dark Hat regularly does the hacking without the authorizations from the directors of the system he is hacking. Yet, he will uncover the system vulnerabilities to the system administrators and offer a fix for the powerlessness for cash.

Script Kiddie: A Script Kiddie is fundamentally a programmer novice who doesn't has much learning to program apparatuses to breaks into PC systems. He regularly utilizes downloaded hacking instruments from web composed by different programmers/security specialists.

Hacktivist: A Hacktivist is a programmer with political goals. The hacktivist has the same abilities as that of a programmer and uses the same instruments as the programmer. The essential aim of a hacktivist is to convey open thoughtfulness regarding a political matter.

Phreaker: Phreaker is a telecom system programmer who hacks a phone framework illicitly to make calls without paying for them.

A programmer is somebody who likes to tinker with hardware or PC frameworks. Programmers like to investigate and figure out how PC frameworks work, discovering approaches to make them improve, or do things they weren't expected to do. There are two sorts of programmers:

White Hat – These are viewed as the great fellows. White hat programmers don't utilize their abilities for unlawful purposes. They typically get to be Computer Security specialists and help shield individuals from the Black Hats.

Black Hat – These are viewed as the awful gentlemen. Black hat programmers for the most part utilize their abilities malevolently for individual increase. They are the individuals that hack banks, take MasterCard's, and damage sites.

These two terms originated from the old western films where the great gentlemen wore white hats and the terrible fellows wore black hats.

Presently in case you're considering, "Oh joy! Being a black hat sounds wonderful!", Then I have an inquiry for you. Does it sound cool to live in a cell the extent of your washroom and be somebody's butt amigo for a long time? That's what I thought.

Programmer Hierarchy

Script kiddies – These are the wannabe programmers. They are looked downward on in the programmer group in light of the fact that they are the individuals that make programmers look awful. Script kiddies for the most part have no hacking abilities and utilize the apparatuses grew by different programmers with no learning of what's occurring off camera.

Middle of the road programmers – These individuals generally think about PCs, organizes, and have enough programming information to see moderately what a script may do, yet like the script kiddies they utilize predeveloped surely understood adventures (- a bit of code that exploits a bug or defenselessness in a bit of programming that permits you to take control of a PC framework) to do assaults

Tip top Hackers – These are the gifted programmers. They are the ones that compose the numerous programmer devices and adventures out there. They can break into frameworks and conceal their tracks or make it seem as though another person did it. You ought to endeavor to in the end achieve this level.

What does it take to turn into a programmer?

Turning into an incredible programmer isn't simple and it doesn't happen rapidly. Being inventive helps a ton. There is more than restricted an issue can be fathomed, and as a programmer you experience numerous issues. The more innovative you are the greater chance you have of hacking a framework without being recognized. Another gigantic quality you must have is the will to learn on the grounds that without it, you will get no place. Keep in mind, Knowledge is force. Persistence is additionally an absolute necessity in light of the fact that numerous subjects can be hard to handle and just after some time will you.

CHAPTER 3: WHY DO PEOPLE HACK?

Myth: Hackers are awful. Really, hackers are simply PC developers who go into another person's code and redesign it some way or another. The term is all around diagramed and characterized by Wikipedia and doesn't straightforwardly allude to anything noxious. An incredible inverse; hackers are software engineers to whom we owe a great deal of much obliged for working out inconveniences in programming and the Internet.

Truth: Hackers really make a case for a Manifesto from 1986 that moves interest and decency and being responsible for one's activities. The proclamation was composed soon after the creator's capture for "Bank Tampering." His best mourn is, "my wrongdoing is that of outflanking you, something that you will never forget me for." Indeed, the weight of being always viewed constrained "The Mentor's" acquiescence in 1990. To all hackers, he is viewed as a living legend.

The Answer: The harm that's done on the Internet and maybe to your PC or your neighbor's PC isn't finished by genuine "hackers." Would you call a graffiti vandal a craftsman or a "painter" in the traditional sense? Little people splash paint structures on the grounds that they can. Infrequently it may feel that it's the best way to leave any imprint with an existence that feels too little for anybody to notice.

Companions see however. The more noteworthy the accomplishment, the more prominent the scope. It's a dim notoriety from a vindictive demonstration with no positive target. YOU weren't intended to experience the ill effects of an assault; the assault was intended to be seen, nonetheless. The primary Internet Worm in history was really a decent test that became systemically incidentally slamming each PC it came in contact with. Numerous pernicious code scholars and "saltines" start sincerely enough simply figuring out how to compose code.

With any learning comes a tipping point where a choice must be made. You in the end improve than the normal individual and ready to do things that curve outside what was intended to happen. Most aptitudes don't abandon one thinking about whether they can harm other individuals' property (the cook doesn't graduate culinary school thinking about whether they ought to harm individuals for instance), yet PC programing uncovers that there's a horrendous parcel of stuff out there that's prepared to break or degenerate with a little push in the wrong heading.

When you figured out how to walk, did you venture on ants? Why? "Since I could; on the grounds that they were there; on the grounds that I needed to; on the grounds that it looked like fun." I'll wager your answer isn't on account of you like harming or slaughtering things. As you developed, you utilized those same feet to take you some place. In time, all the current wafers will develop and in all likelihood get to be splendid individuals from programming society.

There is nobody enchantment answer. It's something that happens and you aren't the objective. You don't comprehend it on the grounds that you don't do it. It is a wrongdoing, yet it's regularly only an adolescent demonstration of poor decision and misled aptitudes. Guard yourself with hostile to infection programming projects, don't succumb to email tricks and realize that some time or another those fiendish feet will be some place great.

After the coming of arranged PCs, there have been hackers who appear to think of it as their own main goal to endeavor those systems. Yet, now, with the interconnectedness (and, consequently, powerlessness) of everything from the gadgets in our pockets to the vehicles we drive, data security dangers are more prominent than at any other time in recent memory some time recently.

Be that as it may, why do hackers do what they do? At the point when the vast majority considers hacking, they imagine delicate data being stolen and utilized for monetary benefit however the fact of the matter is, hacking can spring from a mixture of inspirations.

Inspirations for Hacking

Likewise with any wrongdoing, the variables that rouse exceedingly talented hackers range from individual addition to vision to political plots.

Cutting edge cybersecurity degrees take a gander at these inspirations so understudies can develop their comprehension of where and when digital assaults may strike.

Rush/Challenge

Hackers regularly choose to hack secured frameworks for the same reason mountain climbers feel a compelling desire to climb Mount Everest: in light of the fact that it's there.

Numerous youthful hackers are greatly smart, unmotivated at school due to their insight, and searching for a chance to substantiate themselves. The test of overcoming snags, combined with the rush of knowing they're doing something they aren't permitted to do—and that they've bested another person's security, in this manner demonstrating their predominant capability are once in a while all the inspiration expected to start hacking.

Novice or unaffiliated hackers habitually misuse PCs and systems that are not secret key ensured, seeing such unsecure circumstances as an open welcome to enter. To stay away from recognition, these hackers frequently capture the IP location of another person so that the movement can't be followed back to them.

Help Identify Security Breaches

A few hackers take the rush of the pursuit above and beyond into vigilantism. They trade off the sites and databases of expansive associations for the reasons of recognizing security dangers. Associations utilize these outcomes to enhance their strategies and security.

Associations react to this "help" in a mixture of ways. A few organizations and government associations perceive these endeavors and effectively select from the hacking group to help them recognize and close crevices in security.

Optimism

The different extremist gathering known as Anonymous has been standing out as truly newsworthy for quite a long time by bargaining expansive, secure substances among them abusive outside governments and administrations, national Visa organizations, Wall Street and vast banks, police offices the nation over, even the United States Department of Justice—to challenge anything individuals from the different groups consider improper or harsh.

Since Anonymous is a leaderless gathering, its parameters can't be characterized; visionary hackers from everywhere throughout the globe can guarantee Anonymous connection and sever into cells, starting surges of DDoS (disseminated dissent of administration) assaults in all around composed battles and, sometimes, hacking into and damaging the sites of associations with whom they oppose this idea.

Monetary benefit

Criminal hackers frequently represent monetary profit, either separately or in facilitated gatherings. They can accomplish this in a mixed bag of courses: by introducing malware on individual PCs with a specific end goal to gather passwords to touchy client accounts; by trading off business sites and email frameworks and deceiving clients into giving delicate data; or by specifically hacking into business or government databases to gather charge card numbers or other information of vast quantities of clients all at swoop.

CHAPTER 4: HACKING, INFORMATION PRIVACY, AND LAWS

PC wrongdoing or usually alluded to as Cyber Crime or ICT Crime (van der Merwe, 2008, p.61) is another sort of criminal action which began demonstrating its appalling head in the mid 90's as the Internet turned into a typical spot for online clients around the world. This is because of the way that PC lawbreakers now have the chance to obtain entrance to touchy data in the event that they have the fundamental expertise. This by and large causes colossal issues in the financial circle and results in organizations and people needing to make excessive moves to guarantee their wellbeing and decrease in commission of digital wrongdoing (Gordon, 2000, p.423). Digital wrongdoing or otherwise called PC wrongdoing can be characterized as any criminal action that includes a PC and can be partitioned into two classifications. One, it manages law violations that must be perpetrated which were beforehand impractical before the appearance of the PC, for example, hacking, splitting, sniffing and the generation and obliteration of vindictive code (Ibid) The other classification of PC unlawful acts are much more extensive and have been in presence for quite a long time yet are presently carried out in the digital environment, for example, web misrepresentation, ownership and circulation of kid explicit entertainment to give some examples. It is clear from the over that ICT wrongdoing must be handled with a more complex multi-disciplinary methodology (van der Merwe, 2008, p.61). In current times there is more center from ensuring the "compartment" of assets (the PC is simply the present day likeness a bank vault), just rather than cash or gold it contains information) to securing the genuine resources in most ICT unlawful acts, to be specific the information contained in the PC , the wireless' GPS gadget etc. (van der Merwe, 2008, p.63). The inquiry then normally emerges concerning what sorts of criminal offenses may be perpetrated online and what laws one must apply to charge a wrongdoer to effectively get an arraignment. 2. Basic law position: Prior to the ECT Act

It is presented that preceding the order of the ECT, the normal and statutory law around then could be reached out as generally as would be prudent to cook for the capture and fruitful arraignment of online wrongdoers. One can without much of a stretch apply the basic law wrongdoings of criticism, obscenity (Online youngster erotic entertainment, pulverization of tyke porn), crimeniniuria (otherwise called Cyber-spreading) misrepresentation (Cyber extortion) (S v. Van sanctum Berg 1991 (1) SACR 104 (T)), vanquishing the finishes of equity, scorn of court (as distributed any court procedures without the court's authorization online or by other electronic means), robbery (S v. Harper 1981 (2) SA 638 (D) and S v.Manuel 1953 (4) SA 523 (A) 526 where the court arrived at the conclusion that cash which had been dematerialized could be stolen in its insignificant structure) and falsification to the online types of these offenses. The relevance of the normal law however has its own limits and contracts altogether when managing online wrongdoings including ambush, burglary, coercion, spamming, phishing, injustice, murder, breaking and going into premises with the plan to take and malevolent harm to property.

At the point when taking a gander at the criminal acts of breaking and entering with aim to take and the wrongdoings of malignant harm to property two normally known classes of Computer law violations ring a bell. From one viewpoint, hacking and breaking and then again the creation and dissemination of pernicious code known as infections, worms and Trojan Horses. In S v. Howard (unreported Case no. 41/258/02, Johannesburg local justices court) as examined by Van der Merwe, the court had probably whether the wrongdoing of pernicious harm to property could apply to creating a whole data framework to breakdown. The Court specified further that the wrongdoing no more should have been focused on 'physical property' yet could likewise apply to information messages of information data. (van der Merwe, 2008, p.70). The Interception and Monitoring Act, the Regulation of Interception of Communications and Provision of Communication Related Information Act (RICPCRIA) Act 70 of 2002, the Electronic Communications and Transactions Act and the Promotion of Access to Information Act (PROATIA) for the most part restricts the unlawful capture attempt or checking of any information message which could be utilized as a part of indicting hacker and saltines. 2.1 Interception and Monitoring Prohibition Act The Interception and Monitoring Prohibition Act particularly oversees the observing of transmissions including email. Area 2 expresses that: no individual should – 'purposefully capture or endeavor to block or approve, or secure whatever other individual to catch or to endeavor to block, at wherever in the Republic, any correspondence over the span of its event or transmission'. This implies in basic terms that direct that: (an) Intentionally and without the learning or consent of the dispatcher to block a correspondence which has been or is being or is expected to be transmitted by phone or in whatever other way more than an information transfers line; or

(b) Intentionally screen any discussions or interchanges by method for a checking gadget in order to assemble secret data concerning any individual, body or association, is unlawful and accordingly denied. One must note that the endeavor thereof is as sanctionable as the genuine demonstration of unlawfully catching and observing of an information correspondence. however read the procurement so as not to prohibit some other acknowledged legal grounds of support, for example, need, private guard, legitimate interference, assent, court request or capture attempt mandate. In the English instance of R v. Secretary of State for

Home Department, ex parte Rudduck and others 1987 2 ALL ER 516, the court cautioned that the grounds of legitimization taking into account basic law must be utilized sparingly and must not be promptly accessible as a resistance to the charge of unlawful interference and checking of information interchanges. The scholarly judges talked about the way that there are procurements approving law authorization officers to block and screen information correspondence however the system for getting court orders, prohibit and/or capture and checking mandates (as expressed in the South African law) they must be entirely held fast to as this could bring about a disintegration to the singular's entitlement to protection (see segment 3 (an) and (b) of the RICPCIRA on the procurement with respect to the execution and issuing of interference orders). 2.2 Dangerous Code Now give us a chance to swing to the regular law wrongdoing of vindictive harm to property and how it could identify with hazardous code, for example, Viruses, Worms and Trojan stallions. Unsafe alludes to any PC program that causes devastation or hurt and has been customized in such a route with pernicious plan. Ebersoehn& Henning (2000, p.111) characterizes infection as: 'A bit of programming code normally masked as something else that causes some surprising and , for the casualty typically undesirable occasion and which is regularly composed so it is consequently spread to other PC clients.' They go on further and group them as File infector infections, framework or boot record infections and macro viruses. It must be noticed that infections can either be obliterated or "contracted" by trade of different media or by receipt in an email. Ebersoehn& Henning (2000, p.112) characterize a worm as: 'a sort of an infection... .that arranges itself in a PC framework in a spot where it can do hurt'. The contrast between an infection and a worm is that the previous must be actuated by the client and that worm then again obtains entrance to the PC and quest for other web areas contaminating them simultaneously.

Ebersoehn& Henning characterize a Trojan as:

'A dangerous PC project camouflaged as an amusement, an utility or application.

On a fundamental level, USA regulation and law authorization of Cyber wrongdoing is like that of the EU. In the mid 1980 two essential statutes were gone by UC Congress to battle PC related wrongdoing in which government hobbies are included (Van der Merwe, 2008, p.90), the Counterfeit Access Device and Computer Fraud and Abuse Act (18USC § 1030-1984) and in addition the Electronic Communication Privacy Act (18USC §§ 2500-2711-1986). Digital extortion and making deliberate false representations on the web, (that casualties depend on) is a government offense. Fraud which happens as unapproved utilization of someone else's standardized savings number, driver's permit, work ID or charge card online is likewise a government digital wrongdoing. Lately there was a radical upward takeoff from sentencing rules in conviction for fraud and getting of solutions in addition to other things. Internet betting is for the most part precluded; Nevada State is one of the states that supports of web betting.

Government law that targets senders of spam is constrained to fake telephonic sales or by http://go.warwick.ac.uk/abandon/2009_1/snail 11 Sizwe Snail 28/05/2009 method for electronic structure, yet this is presently being amended. The Federal Trade Commission is not engaged to quit spamming, but rather it may stop false and/or beguiling promoting practices. However the condition of Virginia has taken an activity to explicitly criminal Spam. The unlicensed offer of controlled things online is a digital wrongdoing in the USA. Non-prescriptive and prescriptive medications (e.g. Viagra & Cipro), guns, explosives, cigarettes, liquor and even visas available to be purchased on the web ought to adjust to the terms of the authorizing. However this is all that much an unsettled region of law. A Federal judge dismisses New York's boycott on online cigarette deals as it damages the Federal Commerce Clause.

Kid explicit entertainment, in its different structures, is a government wrongdoing. The offenses incorporate ownership, generation, acquisition, or conveyance or related materials. It is fascinating to take note of the choice of Ashcroft v. Free Speech Coalition (2002) 535 U.S. 234 (2002) in which the Supreme Court judges were split about whether virtual obscene pictures of kids fell afoul of hostile to kid obscenity procurements. Under US law, Cyber-Stalking and Cyber-Harassment has likewise been banned. Reinhardt Buys cited a case of how a wrongdoer expected the personality of a lady in the internet and "solicitated" assault on her benefit by expressing on the web, 'the amount she fantasized of being assaulted' and was liable of accomplice to assault because of his inclusion in the assault. Wrongdoings, for example, hate unlawful acts, murder and homicide dangers are additionally culpable if sure of their components are completed on the web. The utilization of watchword sniffers, conveyance and formation of worm projects and in addition composing of infection projects and Trojan steeds, site ruinations, and web-parodying are additionally no doubt understood government offenses. The No Electronic Theft Act, regarding which it is an offense to swap more than $2,500 in programming, directs typical copyright offenses and copyright administration offenses. The Digital Millennium Copyright Act makes it a wrongdoing to movement in gadgets basically intended for motivation behind dodging innovation assurance measures (against theft gadgets). Different trademark offenses, financial coercion, tax evasion which is done online is likewise viewed as digital wrongdoing and means are as of now being produced to make enactment that can adequately manage these offenses. 6. Conclusion

The greater part of the Cyber-wrongdoing procurements in the ECTA are respectable tries and appear to cover the known sorts of digital wrongdoing. It is reviving to note that the assembly did not make digital criminal acts a dynamic idea of legitimate composition and coherently made wrongdoings that don't just cover wrongdoing after the coming of the PC additionally before the approach of the PC. It is likewise invigorating that the minor endeavor of these unlawful acts additionally constitutes a criminal transgression. South Africa and also nations like Nigeria and Egypt has taken authoritative arms to manage these new law violations. The wrongdoings as expressed in the ECTA are however not excluded from examination. The enforceability of the ECTA procurements are still to be tried in our South African courts and some legitimate professionals and adjudicators (justices and judges) should be instructed and rationally adapted to grasp the digital wrongdoing procurements of the ECTA. Given the borderless waythe internet and the challenges it poses in terms of jurisdictional questions, international co-operation and uniformity, it is of the utmost importance that States learn from each other's efforts to deal with Cyber-crime and create an international Cyber-crime code to be applied universally if any significant success is to be achieved in combating Cyber-crime.

CHAPTER 5: PROTECTING YOURSELF

Many of us have openly welcomed the internet into our lives.

For most of us the internet is part of our daily routine for keeping in touch with friends and family, working, studying, playing games, shopping and paying bills.

While the internet offers us many benefits, there are also a range of safety and security risks associated with its use.

These include threats to the integrity of our identities, our privacy and

the security of our electronic communications, in particular financial transactions, as well as exposure to offensive and illegal content and behavior.

Reduce your risk

Being aware of what risks you face online will help you make informed choices about how you use the internet.

There are no absolute guarantees that you can protect all of your information online – but by following the advice in this book you can significantly reduce your risk of becoming a victim of cyber crime.

A bit unsure?

Taking the necessary steps to protect yourself online can be a bit daunting – especially to those less familiar with technology or the internet. However, there are simple steps you can take to protect yourself and your family online.

By taking the time to understand online risks and how to minimize them, you can gain greater confidence in how to be safe and secure when using the internet.

This book provides a range of information to help protect you online:

- 8 simple tips that you should always follow
- Further information on various online issues, including basic steps that you are strongly encouraged to take
- Some sections of this book also provide additional information, for those who wish to take further precautions.

Mobile computing is now a dominant trend. While the term 'computer' is used throughout this document it's important to remember that your phone, tablet computer, game console and even refrigerator may be able to connect to the internet. The processing power in these devices and the amount of personal information they hold is equivalent to a small computer so only thinking about security for 'computers' misses the reality of the modern world.

Read on to find out what you need to know to help protect yourself and your family online.

You can also refer to the glossary at the end of this book to help you understand some online terms, including those marked throughout this book.

There are a lot of steps you can take to protect yourself online – and it can seem a bit complicated, especially if you are new to using the internet.

This booklet provides a range of information to cater for you – no matter whether you have had a little or a lot of experience online.

Whether you are new to using the internet or a regular user – there are 8 simple tips that you need to follow to help protect yourself online:

What these steps show is that protecting yourself online is about more than just how you set up and use your computer, mobile phone or any internet enabled device. It's also about being smart in what you do and the choices you make while using the internet.

There are criminals who use the anonymity of the internet to run old and new scams. While many of these are scams that most people would spot a mile away if they were attempted in the 'real' world, online scams are very sophisticated and often harder to detect.

So it's important to remember that while the technology may be new, the old wisdom still applies. If something you see online or which is sent to you seems suspicious or too good to be true, it probably is.

Further information about online issues and the steps you can take to be safe online are provided in the following chapters.

How to secure your computer
Average time it takes to attack an unprotected computer connected to the internet is measured in minutes.1

So it's important to protect your computer properly. Otherwise you may be putting yourself and possibly your family and friends at risk.

Make sure your computer is protected from harmful emails and viruses, and from unauthorized people accessing your internet connection and personal information.

Install security software

To help secure your computer you need reputable security software. The easiest software to install is an all-in-one package that includes virus and malware protection, spyware protection, a firewall – and parental controls

if you have children. If you're not sure what software is reputable ask at your local computer store or look for IT magazine or online surveys of security software.

Here are some basic steps you can take to secure your computer

- install reputable security software that protects your computer from viruses, malware and spyware, and includes a firewall
- have your security software set to update automatically
- Renew your security software when the subscription is due.

Also, beware of scareware – these are pop-up messages or unsolicited emails that tell you that your computer is compromised and want you to purchase software to repair it. These messages aim to trick users into believing your computer is already infected, and that purchasing the software will help get rid of it. Checking your security settings and making sure your pop-up blocker is on may help avoid this. There have also been instances where users have received a phone call purporting to be from a security company advising them that their computer is at risk. Quite often the message and the software are fake.

Turn on programmed upgrades

Respectable programming organizations frequently issue free overhauls to their product to settle security and different issues. These fixes are called patches, and they ought to for the most part be connected when they're accessible. Security fixes are additionally included as a rule redesigns, regardless of the fact that they don't say it.

Most programming will have a choice called 'check for redesigns' under the help drop-down menu. You should check this frequently. A ton of working framework and application programming can now be set to redesign naturally – you ought to empower this alternative wherever it is accessible.

Utilize a standard client account

Your PC has two sorts of client record choices, a standard or regulatory record. Making and utilizing a standard client represent most day by day assignments, for example, surfing the web and perusing messages, will diminish the sum and sort of malware that has the capacity contaminate your PC.

Numerous types of genuine malware oblige a client to be running a manager record so as to effectively contaminate your PC. Running online with a standard client account significantly decreases the viability of numerous sorts of malware. To discover more.

Set and secure your passwords

Passwords aren't totally unbreakable, yet they can help keep lawbreakers from getting to your PC.

Here are some essential steps you can take to set and ensure your secret words

- choose an "in number" watchword
  - a least of eight characters
  - a blend of upper and lower case letters
  - at slightest one number, and

- at slightest one image
- avoid utilizing words found as a part of the dictionary

- have different passwords for different activities and change them regularly, particularly those for sensitive transactions such as banking, social networking and your computer logon

- don't store a list of your passwords on your computer in a word document – this makes it easy for anyone who gets into your computer to access your social networking, banking and other accounts

- Select 'no' when your computer offers to automatically remember a password when logging into a website, especially banking, social networking and web mail accounts. This is because scammers can use malware to find these stored within the PC.

- If it helps to write your passwords down, do so – but hide them somewhere safe, away from prying eyes and not together with your computer logon. An even better idea is to use a passphrase.

Utilization of shrewd settings for your web program

A web program is the product you use to view sites.

Try not to utilize the "recollect" capacity for passwords that offer access to budgetary or individual data like your keeping money or person to person communication accounts. This guarantees that if your web program gets assaulted, you don't lose the greater part of your delicate passwords.

Most PCs accompany a web program officially introduced. Then again, there is no assurance that the web program has been set up with the right security settings for your needs. Hackers know how to adventure web program settings, so it's vital to choose the right settings to secure your own data.

The higher you set your security levels, the less choices and capacities you will have accessible, yet the more secure your web access will be. You need to choose the right adjust for you between being as secure as would be prudent and encountering each element of each site.

Your program's security capacities can for the most part be found in one of the drop-down menu things. Most programs give exhortation on each of the security settings and clarify the favorable circumstances and burdens of empowering or handicapping capacities and high and low security settings.

Here are some essential steps you can take when setting up your web program

- Set up your own security settings on your web program
- If in uncertainty – set the security levels to high. However, realize that this may limit your capacity to view and utilize a few sites or the capacities on them
- Use the most recent form – so overhaul your web program as new forms get to be accessible.

Control your web association

More Australians are associating with the web utilizing a broadband association, whether it is ADSL, remote or link.

Notwithstanding desktop PCs and tablets, numerous cell phones, for example, advanced cells, can be utilized to get to the web. It's pretty much as critical to empower security settings for advanced mobile phones, or whatever other gadget with web integration – especially where it contains private or touchy data.

Here are some fundamental steps you can take to control your web association

- Use an in number secret key to ensure physical access to any gadget that holds individual data on it –, for example, PCs, PDAs, and switches
- Always kill your web association when you feel ur not safe.

- If you have an ADSL or remote modem then you ought to dependably change the default secret key.

For more data weigh the guidelines in the producer's handbook or ask your Internet Service Provider (ISP) for exhortation.

Some extra steps you can take to control your web associations are:

- Set up discrete records – just get to the web by utilizing a record with constrained access, as opposed to by an executive record.
- Here are some essential steps you can take to secure your PDA and its web association
- Use a PIN or secret word, so nobody can get to your private information if your telephone is lost or stolen

- Like your PC, set programmed redesigns or check consistently for downloads to your telephone's working framework and applications
- Only download applications from authority stores or from a trusted source, for example, your own bank
- Take control of your PDA - kill your Wi-Fi and Bluetooth when not being used or change your settings so that your telephone requests authorization to join other remote systems.
- Only associate your telephone to a safe (encoded) remote system keeping in mind it's okay for general scanning don't utilize open remote systems for imperative online exchanges, for example, managing an account
- Be cautious about how you permit your telephone to show your area –, for example, GPS applications. Do you truly need a cheat to know where you live and when your home is unfilled?

- Tampering with your telephone's product or working framework (at times known as jail breaking) may abandon it presented to extra security vulnerabilities

Secure your remote system

Remote systems are an extraordinary approach to make the web more open and to share data between gadgets on the web.

Be that as it may, an unsecured system is much the same as an unprotected PC – it leaves your own and monetary data helpless. Securing your remote association can keep obscure individuals from getting to your remote association for unnecessary downloads or unlawful exercises.

In the event that you run a remote system at home or in your business there are a couple steps you have to take to make it secure.

Here are some essential steps you can take to control your remote system

- Assign a secret word so that any gadget that is joined to the system must know the watchword to join. Don't simply utilize the default passwords as these are broadly known and verify you utility
- Change the Service Set Identifier (SSID), the name that identifies the wireless network. Don't use a name that makes your network easy for others to identify, such as your family's name or business name
- Make sure your network encryption is turned on and, just like your software, use the latest encryption available on the device.
- If you are unsure of how to do this follow the instructions in the manufacturer's handbook or seek advice from your ISP.

The strides plot in the past area are an imperative begin in securing yourself on the web. Then again, basically setting up and keeping up your PC effectively is insufficient to completely ensure yourself and your family and companions.

You likewise should be savvy about what you do and the decisions you make on the web. This implies being mindful of potential dangers while executing on the web, especially where cash is included. It's critical to indicate matter of fact and not be deceived into doing things online that you wouldn't feel great doing in the "genuine" world.

Counteract infections and other malware

Noxious programming or malware is a bland term for programming that is intended to explicitly harm, disturb or take control of frameworks.

Sorts of malware incorporate things, for example, infections, Trojans, worms or spyware.

Your PC can be contaminated by malware through email messages, going to traded off sites, and downloading tainted records.

Here are some fundamental strides to anticipate malware

- Scan email connections with security programming before opening them
- Don't open messages or connections in case you're not expecting them or you don't have the foggiest idea about the sender
- think precisely before you tap on connections and connections in messages and on person to person communication destinations
- Only download records from sites you trust
- double watch that the URL or site location is right, as the connection may divert you towards a fake

location, which may seem to be like the honest to goodness site

- Be attentive when trading documents over systems
- Read the permit understanding and terms of utilization before you download programming and don't download it in the event that you don't believe the terms and conditions
- Never tap on a 'Concur', "alright" or "No" catch to close a window on a site you don't trust. This can dispatch spyware onto your PC. Rather, tap the red "X" tab to close the window.

Computer hackers are on the loose worldwide. Big and small companies as well as individuals are easy targets. The mighty Google's recent revelation that it servers have been attacked by hackers, and that Chinese, US and European human rights activists have been adversely affected is proof that hackers are cause for concern. They take delight in discovering the vulnerabilities in your computer system and are indiscriminate agents of destruction.

Enticements to open a malicious email attachment or visit a malicious email attachment or visit a malicious website abound. Once opened, hidden codes allow a remote user to quietly take and retain control of your computer until it is detected or removed.

Here are a few things you can do to help protect your computer from hackers:-

1. Adobe Acrobat Reader and Flash Player are not always safe to use; however if you have to use them for your work please ensure you have the latest version appropriate to your work.

2. Install and update anti-virus and anti-malware software, checking for regular system patches from your vendor (e.g. Apple or Microsoft). Use common sense when opening attachments.

3. Never use an account with administrative privileges for ordinary work, particularly

email or online activities such as web surfing.

4. Program your computer to "go to sleep" after a short period of inactivity and require a password to wake it up again.

5. Activate the firewall built-in to your system. Check your documentation or online help for instructions on how to do this.

6. When a new version of an operating system comes out, delete the old one first before installing the new. This ensures you have a "clean" system going forward.

7. Consider purchasing an email digital ID. When you send an email this will allow the recipient to authenticate your identity and allow you to encrypt the contents of your message.

8. Run a proper "scanning" program on a regular basis.

9. Remember, hackers like to look for "security holes" through which they can gain entry without much trouble. These

holes frequently exist in the programs and plug-ins that we install on our sites.

10. New software vulnerabilities are found all the time and sometime attacks are devised before software vendors even become aware of the vulnerabilities or patch them. Your best defenses are caution and vigilance.

CHAPTER 6: THE HACKER MINDSET

This investigates how understanding the mentality of a hacker and the approach they utilize to adventure frameworks can help security specialists in enhancing the security of programming frameworks. It looks all the more profoundly at a percentage of the specialized parts of the hacking process and endeavors to present them in a manner that is justifiable to somebody without much programming or PC experience.

"Hackers assault Microsoft PCs" [1], "Mac PCs "hacked" in rupture" [2], "Facebook was focused by "complex" hackers" [3]. These and comparative features have been circling in the news in the course of recent months. Organizations in every industry have all as of late conceded to having their PC frameworks broken by unapproved clients. A few individuals have even begun calling 2013 "The Year of the Hack" . The inquiry that the vast majority are asking is:

how did all these apparently secure frameworks get to be traded off? While it may be critical to take a gander at the particular vulnerabilities in programming that hackers had the capacity sidestep in request to decide how they were traded off, more must be done so as to avert such assaults later on. Eventually, inspecting the outlook and system of hackers: their state of mind, aptitudes, and assault system is basic to enhancing the security of software.

The Hacker Mindset: Attitude and Skills

While the hacker subculture developed out of a yearning to comprehend PC frameworks and adoration for programming [6], it has subsequent to developed into something that is viler. Today, hackers are inspired by a longing to pick up cash from their endeavors. With the expanding measure of data that is set onto PCs and the expanding measure of business that is being directed through PCs and on the web, hackers have more open doors than any other time in recent memory to benefit from taking delicate information from PC frameworks. In any case, keeping in mind the end goal to do this, hackers should be more than only specialists at PC programming.

While the regular generalization of a hacker is a geek who sits at their PC throughout the day composing programming to break into PC frameworks, without a doubt hackers need both PC programming and social building aptitudes to succeed. As opposed to misusing shortcomings in the product frameworks, social building makes utilization of the way that people can be controlled to unveil data or permit access to things they are attempting to ensure given the right inspiration [7]. It includes a hacker utilizing human brain science and how people act keeping in mind the end goal to delude the casualty into uncovering data that may be valuable in picking up access to their PCs. For instance, phishing is a typical sample of social designing that endeavors to increase private data, (for example, passwords and Visa numbers) from somebody by professing to be a trusted individual or corporation.1 One illustration of a phishing assault is a hacker taking on the appearance of a client's bank and requesting that the client send their record data in light of the fact that deceitful action was apparently recognized on it, when actually the hacker is simply attempting to take the record data. [Multimedia: sample of a phishing email or site with callouts demonstrating diverse key parts of the email] The essential part that social building plays in all phases of a hacker's assault can't be overlooked. Stages of an Attack

Keeping in mind the end goal to really break into a framework, hackers by and large take after an anticipated arrangement of steps:

Surveillance/Information Gathering, Scanning/Vulnerability Identification, Exploitation, and Looking after Access/Covering Tracks. While these strides are regularly taken after directly, they can likewise be more cyclic in nature, as hackers may participate in further surveillance or examining subsequent to endeavoring numerous fizzled adventures.

Surveillance

The main step, surveillance, includes assembling as much data about the objective as conceivable so as to distinguish potential strategies to assault them. There are two fundamental sorts of observation: aloof and dynamic. Uninvolved surveillance endeavors to get data about the planned server(s) without cautioning them to the attacker's vicinity. One of the simplest and most regular strategies for doing this is by utilizing internet searchers as a part of request to discover data about the association, for example, the foundation of the organization, worker logins, also, other evidently private data. Case in point, numerous organizations utilize the neighborhood part of a worker's email deliver as their login to PC frameworks (e.g. a client with email john @ organization . com will have a username of "john"). In the event that a hacker has the capacity take in the email locations of workers, they then know potential logins. Active observation, then again, is significantly more forceful and can thusly be recognized all the more effortlessly by components that are intended to anticipate hacking. What recognizes dynamic observation from detached surveillance is the way that dynamic observation speaks specifically with PC servers that may be possessed by the casualty, rather than utilizing instruments, for example, web indexes which are unaffiliated with the objective. One essential part of dynamic observation is finding the IP locations of the objective servers.

An IP address extraordinarily recognizes any PC on the Internet, like how a road address recognizes any building. Hackers utilization devices, for example, nslookup to decipher from a host name of a web server (e.g. www .examplesite . com) to its IP address (e.g. 192.168.1.1) so that they can complete more mind boggling assaults against that particular PC.

Filtering

After observation, penetration analyzers use different checking systems to recognize vulnerabilities inside of the found frameworks. Two related checking strategies are port checking and weakness filtering. Port checking endeavors to locate the open system ports on a server. System ports are utilized by PCs to correspond with each other more than a system then again the Internet. By sending messages to ports on a casualty's PC, a hacker can figure out whether a port is "open", "shut", or "sifted". Open ports are those ports which can acknowledge approaching associations. For example, corporate web servers for the most part have a port open so that individuals can utilize a program to associate and perspective the organization site. Shut ports, then again, are those ports on the server that are not tolerating approaching correspondence. At last, separated ports will be ports that may be open or shut, yet some protective security measure, for example, a firewall, keeps the hacker from deciding its real state. By deciding which ports are open on an objective PC, hackers have the capacity to identify conceivable "doors" into that computer.Exploitation In the wake of deciding potential vulnerabilities, the analyzer or hacker endeavors to misuse these shortcomings keeping in mind the end goal to obtain entrance to the framework. By sending particular summons or bits of PC code to the defenseless ports found in the past step, an attacker may have the capacity to obtain entrance to the file system of the PC and execute programs on the casualty's machine.

Different comparable vulnerabilities exist in various programming applications and may hence be simpler to discover and misuse. For instance, a support flood is a typical defenselessness that happens at the point when a system acknowledges client enter and does not check the length of the info before endeavoring to store it in PC memory (a "cushion"). On the off chance that the information string is too long, it "floods" out of the size of the cradle, overwriting different parts of PC memory that were not planned to be changed, which can harm the system or permit the hacker to execute their own PC code rather than the code of the first program However, not all types of misuse include the hacker straightforwardly connecting with the casualty's

PC, attempting to discover shortcomings in its safeguards. Hackers frequently make programming projects called "malware" that can be utilized to abuse various casualties. Malware can be characterized as "code or programming that is particularly intended to harm, upset, take, or as a rule dispense some other "awful" or illegitimate activity on information, has, or systems" [9]. Making and appropriating malware regularly depends upon the social designing aptitudes of the hacker, as they must discover approaches to attempt to persuade clients that the noxious programming they are running is safe. For instance, a hacker may advertize that they have different "free screensaver" records on their site, yet when those records are downloaded they are really pernicious and taint the client's PC. It is imperative to note that there are really distinctive sorts of malware, as not all malware demonstrations in the same way or fills the same need. For example, one sort of malware is an infection.

Albeit numerous individuals casually allude to any sort of malware as an infection, an infection is really a subset of malware. It comprises of PC code that is "self-repeating", being able to duplicate itself into the current code of an alternate PC system, "tainting" that program. Once it contaminates the new program, at whatever point that program is currently run, the replication procedure rehashes

Despite the fact that replication without anyone else is not so much destructive, an infection might likewise perform other undesirable activities on the casualty's PC. Case in point, an infection may endeavor to transfer client documents to the attacker or download different sorts of malware on the machine, for example, spyware, in request to take client data. This data can be of different structures, for example, usernames, passwords, web-seeing history, or money related data, (for example, ledgers or MasterCard numbers). In the wake of gathering data from the casualty PC, the spyware then transmits this information back to a server, in a procedure known as "calling home", so that the attacker

Initially, "hacking" implied a rich, witty or roused method for doing practically anything.

In this session, you will figure out how a hacker's attitude can show you to acknowledge what is conceivable.

Key Points

- Hacking is more than simply something insidious tech nerds accomplish for no particular reason and benefit: it is a propensity for brain that lights advancement and motivates creation
- The play area of hackers is not constrained to the domain of PCs and the Internet: it includes almost all gadgets, from ordinary bolts and keys to cars and cell phones
- Forward-speculation companies ought to consider taking hackers out of PC security divisions and putting them in item advancement divisions

Outline

Pablos Holman is a self-portrayed "white hat hacker" – that is, one who puts his hacking aptitudes to use to teach associations about system security instead of wreak ruin in the internet and purloin touchy information. In a vivacious also, educational session, Holman outlined only a percentage of the numerous security vulnerabilities that encompass individuals in their regular lives, exhibiting the simplicity with which hackers can control remote auto keys, arranged inn room TV frameworks, cell systems' phone message frameworks, Bluetooth-empowered gadgets and MasterCard's containing RFID chips.

Holman is likewise an innovator, who outfits the extremely same out-of-the-crate thinking and irrepressible interest that urges him to hack to concoct imaginative answers for a percentage of the world's more recalcitrant issues.

Holman and his associates at Intellectual Ventures Labs, established by previous Microsoft CTO Nathan Myhrvold, are presently giving their mechanical ability and diverse personalities to fascinating tasks: systems of monster, ocean borne rings produced using reused truck tires, that saddle wave vitality to push the warm surface descending to lessen warm air updrafts that make sea tempests; utilizing hoses borne overhead by helium blow ups to shower sulfur dioxide into

the upper environment to emulate the impact of volcanic movement with expectations of switching the retreat of the Arctic ice top; what's more, an innovation to reuse the a great many huge amounts of atomic waste made by atomic plants and weapons programs for force era.

Where non-hackers ordinarily take a gander at a gadget – a cell telephone, for occurrence – and comprehends it as far as "what does this gadget do", the hacker has a striking resemblance gadget and asks, "What would I be able to make this gadget do?" Holman accepts that this mentality is absolutely what is expected to start development and creation. Also, it is likewise the attitude required in the World Economic Forum's progressing endeavors to reexamine, update.

CHAPTER 7: PLANNING ATTACKS (HOW YOU'LL GO ABOUT IT & WHAT YOU PLAN ON TAKING)

How Hackers Beget Ethical Hackers

We've all known about hackers. A considerable lot of us have even endured the outcomes of hacker activities. So who are these hackers? Why is it imperative to think about them? The following few areas give you the lowdown on hackers.

Characterizing hackers

Hacker is a word that has two implications:

1. Traditionally, a hacker is somebody who likes to tinker with programming or electronic frameworks. Hackers appreciate investigating and figuring out how PC frameworks work. They cherish

finding better approaches to work electronically.

2. Recently, hacker has tackled another importance — somebody who malignantly breaks into frameworks for individual increase. In fact, these hoodlums are wafers (criminal hackers). Wafers break into (split) frameworks with vindictive goal. They are out for individual increase: acclaim, benefit, and even retribution. They change, erase, and take discriminating data, frequently making other individuals hopeless.

The great gentleman (white-hat) hackers don't care for being in the same class as the awful fellow (black-hat) hackers. (These terms originate from Western motion pictures where the great gentlemen wore white cattle rustler hats and the terrible fellows wore black cowhand hats.) Whatever the case, the vast majority give hacker a negative intention.

Numerous noxious hackers assert that they don't bring about harm however rather are selflessly helping other people. Definitely, right. Numerous malignant hackers are electronic criminals.

In this book, I utilize the accompanying phrasing:

1. Hackers (or awful fellows) attempt to bargain PCs.

2. Ethical hackers (or great gentlemen) secure PCs against unlawful passage.

Hackers go for any framework they think they can bargain. Some lean toward prestigious, very much ensured frameworks, however hacking into anybody's framework builds their status in hacker circles.

Ethical Hacking 101

You require insurance from hacker shenanigans. An ethical hacker has what it takes, outlook, and devices of a hacker but on the other hand is reliable. Ethical hackers perform the hacks as security tests for their frameworks.

On the off chance that you perform ethical hacking tests for clients or essentially need to add another affirmation to your accreditations, you may need to consider the ethical hacker accreditation Certified Ethical Hacker, which is supported by EC-Council. See www.eccouncil.org/CEH.htm for more data.

Ethical hacking — otherwise called penetration testing or white-hat hacking — includes the same instruments, traps, and methods that hackers use, however with one noteworthy distinction: Ethical hacking is legitimate. Ethical hacking is performed with the objective's authorization. The aim of ethical hacking is to find vulnerabilities from a hacker's perspective so frameworks can be better secured. It's a piece of a general data hazard administration program that considers progressing security upgrades. Ethical hacking can likewise guarantee that sellers' cases about the security of their items are honest to goodness.

To hack your own particular frameworks like the awful fellows, you must think like they think. It's totally discriminating to know your adversary; see Chapter 2 for subtle elements.

Understanding the Need to Hack Your Own Systems

To catch a cheat, take on a similar mindset as a hoodlum. That's the premise for ethical hacking.

The theory of probability conflicts with security. With the expanded numbers and extending information of hackers joined with the developing number of framework vulnerabilities and different questions, the time will come when every single PC framework are hacked or traded off somehow. Shielding your frameworks from the terrible gentlemen — and not simply the non specific vulnerabilities that everybody thinks about — is completely discriminating. When you know hacker deceives, you can perceive how powerless your frameworks are.

Hacking preys on frail security rehearses and undisclosed vulnerabilities. Firewalls, encryption, and virtual private systems (VPNs) can make a bogus feeling of security. These security frameworks regularly concentrate on abnormal state vulnerabilities, for example, infections and activity through a firewall, without influencing how hackers work. Assaulting your own frameworks to find vulnerabilities is a stage to making them more secure. This is the main demonstrated technique for significantly solidifying your frameworks from assault. On the off chance that you don't recognize shortcomings, it's a matter of time before the vulnerabilities are misused.

As hackers extend their insight, so if you. You must think like them to shield your frameworks from them. You, as the ethical hacker, must know exercises hackers complete and how to stop their endeavors. You ought to comprehend what to search for and how to utilize that data to obstruct hackers' endeavors.

You don't need to shield your frameworks from everything. You can't. The main insurance against everything is to unplug your PC frameworks and lock them away so nobody can touch them — not even you. That's not the best way to deal with data security. What's essential is to ensure your systems from known vulnerabilities and normal hacker assaults.

It's difficult to support every conceivable vulnerabilities on every one of your frameworks. You can't get ready for every single conceivable assault — particularly the ones that are right now obscure. Then again, the more blends you attempt — the more you test entire frameworks rather than individual units — the better your shots of finding vulnerabilities that influence everything in general.

Try not to take ethical hacking too far, however. It looks bad to solidify your frameworks from far-fetched assaults. Case in point, on the off chance that you don't have a considerable measure of pedestrian activity in your office and no interior Web server running, you might not have as much to stress over as an Internet facilitating supplier would have. Notwithstanding, bear in mind about insider dangers from malevolent workers!

Your general objectives as an ethical hacker ought to be as per the following:

1. Hack your frameworks in a nondestructive manner.
2. Enumerate vulnerabilities and, if essential, demonstrate to upper administration that vulnerabilities exist.
3. Apply results to uproot vulnerabilities and better secure your frameworks. Understanding the Dangers Your Systems Face

It's one thing to realize that your frameworks for the most part are under flame from hackers around the globe. It's another to comprehend particular assaults against your systems that are conceivable. This area offers some no doubt understood assaults yet is in no way, shape or form an extensive posting. That obliges its own particular book: Hack Attacks Encyclopedia, by John Chirillo (Wiley Publishing, Inc.).

Numerous data security vulnerabilities aren't basic without anyone else's input. On the other hand, misusing a few vulnerabilities in the meantime can take its toll. Case in point, a default Windows OS design, a frail SQL Server administrator watchword, and a server facilitated on a remote system may not be real security concerns independently. Be that as it may, abusing every one of the three of these vulnerabilities in the meantime can be a significant issue.

Nontechnical assaults

Abuses that include controlling individuals —
end clients and even yourself — are the best
powerlessness inside of any PC or system base.
People are trusting by nature, which can prompt
social-designing endeavors. Social designing is
characterized as the misuse of the trusting way of
people to pick up data for vindictive purposes. I
cover social designing inside and out in Chapter
5.

Other regular and compelling assaults against
data frameworks are physical. Hackers break
into structures, PC rooms, or different ranges
containing critical data or property. Physical
assaults can incorporate dumpster plunging
(scrounging through waste jars and dumpsters
for licensed innovation, passwords, system
outlines, and other data).

System foundation assaults

Hacker assaults against system foundations can
be simple, in light of the fact that numerous

systems can be come to from anyplace on the planet through the Internet. Here are a few illustrations of system framework assaults:

1. Connecting into a system through a rebel modem appended to a PC behind a firewall
2. Exploiting shortcomings in system transport systems, for example, TCP/IP and NetBIOS
3. Flooding a system with an excess of solicitations, making a disavowal of administration (DoS) for honest to goodness demands
4. Installing a system analyzer on a system and catching each parcel that goes crosswise over it, uncovering secret data in clear content
5. Piggybacking onto a system through a frail 802.

Working framework assaults

Hacking working frameworks (OSs) is a favored system for the awful fellows. OSs involve a huge bit of hacker assaults basically on the grounds that each PC has one thus some no doubt understood adventures can be utilized against them.

Sometimes, some working frameworks that are more secure out of the case —, for example, Novell NetWare and the kinds of BSD UNIX — are assaulted, and vulnerabilities turn up. In any case, hackers incline toward assaulting working frameworks like Windows and Linux in light of the fact that they are generally utilized and better known for their vulnerabilities.

Here are a few illustrations of assaults on working frameworks:

v Exploiting particular convention usage

v Attacking inherent verification frameworks

v Breaking record framework security

v Cracking passwords and encryption systems

Application and other particular assaults

Applications take a considerable measure of hits by hackers. Projects, for example, email server programming and Web applications frequently are pounded:

v Hypertext Transfer Protocol (HTTP) and Simple Mail Transfer Protocol (SMTP) applications are as often as possible assaulted on the grounds that most firewalls and other security instruments are arranged to permit full access to these projects from the Internet.

v Malicious programming (malware) incorporates infections, worms, Trojan stallions, and spyware. Malware stops up systems and brings down frameworks.

v Spam (garbage email) is wreaking devastation on framework accessibility and storage room. What's more, it can convey malware.

Ethical hacking helps uncover such assaults against your PC frameworks. Parts II through V of this book cover these assaults in subtle element, alongside specific countermeasures you can actualize against assaults on your frameworks.

Complying with the Ethical Hacking Commandments

Each ethical hacker must keep a couple of essential charges. If not, terrible things can happen. I've seen these rules disregarded or overlooked when arranging or executing ethical hacking tests. The outcomes weren't certain.

Working ethically

The word ethical in this connection can be characterized as living up to expectations with high professional ethics and standards. Whether you're performing ethical hacking tests against your own particular frameworks or for somebody who has procured you, all that you do as an ethical hacker must be candid and must bolster the organization's objectives. No shrouded plans are permitted!

Dependability is a definitive fundamental. The abuse of data is totally illegal. That's what the terrible fellows do.

Regarding protection

Treat the data you accumulate with the most extreme appreciation. All data you acquire amid your testing — from Web-application log documents to clear-message passwords — must be kept private. Try not to utilize this data to snoop into classified corporate data or private lives. In the event that you sense that somebody ought to know there's an issue, consider offering that data to the suitable director.

Include others in your procedure. This is a "watch the watcher" framework that can construct trust and backing your ethical hacking activities.

Not slamming your frameworks

One of the greatest slip-ups I've seen when individuals attempt to hack their own systems is unintentionally smashing their frameworks. The fundamental explanation behind this is lack of foresight. These analyzers have not read the documentation or misjudge the use and force of the security instruments and strategies.

You can undoubtedly make DoS conditions on your frameworks when testing. Running an excess of tests too rapidly on a framework causes numerous framework lockups. I know on the grounds that I've done this! Try not to surge things and expect that a system or specific host can deal with the beating that system scanners and weakness appraisal apparatuses can hand out.

Numerous security-evaluation instruments can control what number of tests are performed on a framework in the meantime. These instruments are particularly convenient in the event that you have to run the tests on generation frameworks amid consistent business hours.

You can even make a record or framework lockout condition by social engineering somebody into changing a secret key, not understanding that doing as such may make a framework lockout condition.

The Ethical Hacking Process

Like for all intents and purposes any IT or security venture, ethical hacking should be arranged ahead of time. Key and strategic issues in the ethical hacking procedure ought to be resolved and settled upon. Arranging is essential for any measure of testing — from a straightforward secret word splitting test to a hard and fast penetration test on a Web application.

Defining your arrangement

Approbation for ethical hacking is crucial. Make what you're doing known and obvious — in any event to the leaders. Getting sponsorship of the venture is the first step. This could be your director, an official, a client, or even yourself in case you're the supervisor. You require somebody to back you up and approve your arrangement. Something else, your testing may be canceled suddenly in the event that somebody guarantees they never approved you to perform the tests.

The approval can be as straightforward as an inside notice from your manager in case you're performing these tests all alone frameworks. In case you're testing for a client, have a marked contract set up, expressing the client's backing and approval. Get composed regard on this sponsorship as quickly as time permits to guarantee that none of your time or exertion is squandered. This documentation is your Get Out of Jail Free card if anybody questions what you're doing.

You require an itemized arrangement, however that doesn't mean you need to have volumes of testing methodology. One slip can crash your frameworks — not so much what anybody needs. A very much characterized extension incorporates the accompanying data:

v Specific frameworks to be tried

v Risks that are included

v When the tests are performed and your general course of events

v How the tests are performed

v How much information of the frameworks you have before you begin testing

v What is done when a noteworthy weakness is found

v The particular deliverables — this incorporates security-appraisal reports and a more elevated amount report plotting the general vulnerabilities to be tended to, alongside countermeasures that ought to be executed

At the point when selecting frameworks to test, begin with the most discriminating or defenseless frameworks. For example, you can test PC passwords or endeavor social-designing assaults before penetrating down into more itemized frameworks.

It pays to have an alternate course of action for your ethical hacking process on the off chance that something goes amiss. What in case you're evaluating your firewall or Web application, and you bring it down? This can bring about framework inaccessibility, which can lessen framework execution or worker efficiency. Much more terrible, it could bring about loss of information respectability, loss of information, and awful reputation.

Handle social-building and refusal of-administration assaults painstakingly. Decide how they can influence the frameworks you're testing and your whole association.

Deciding when the tests are performed is something that you must take some real time to contemplate. Do you test amid ordinary business hours? What about late around evening time or at a young hour in the morning so that creation frameworks aren't influenced? Include others to verify they endorse of your timing.

The best approach is a boundless assault, wherein any kind of test is possible. The awful gentlemen aren't hacking your frameworks inside of a constrained degree, so why would it be advisable for you to? A few exemptions to this methodology are performing DoS, social-building, and physical-security tests.

Try not to stop with one security gap. This can prompt an incorrect feeling that all is well with the world. Continue going to see what else you can find. I'm not saying to continue hacking until the end of time or until you crash every one of your frameworks. Essentially seek after the way you're going down until you can't hack it any more (play on words proposed).

One of your objectives may be to perform the tests without being distinguished. For instance, you may be performing your tests on remote frameworks or on a remote office, and you don't need the clients to be mindful of what you're doing. Other-wise, the clients may be on to you and be on their best conduct.

You needn't bother with broad learning of the frameworks you're testing — only an essential comprehension. This will help you ensure the tried frameworks.

Understanding the frameworks you're testing shouldn't be troublesome in case you're hacking your own in-house frameworks. In case you're hacking a client's frameworks, you may need to burrow more profound. Actually, I've never had a client request a completely daze evaluation. A great many people are terrified of these evaluations. Base the kind of test you will perform on your association's or client needs.

Selecting instruments

Likewise with any undertaking, in the event that you don't have the right instruments for ethical hacking, accomplishing the assignment successfully is troublesome. Having said that, simply in light of the fact that you utilize the right apparatuses doesn't imply that you will find all vulnerabilities.

Know the individual and specialized constraints. Numerous security-evaluation instruments produce false positives and negatives (erroneously distinguishing vulnerabilities). Others may miss vulnerabilities. In case you're performing tests, for example, social-designing or physical-security appraisals, you may miss shortcomings.

Numerous devices concentrate on particular tests, yet nobody apparatus can test for everything. For the same reason that you wouldn't drive in a nail with a screwdriver, you shouldn't utilize a word processor to check your system for open ports. This is the reason you require an arrangement of particular instruments that you can approach for the current workload. The more apparatuses you have, the less demanding your ethical hacking endeavors are.

Verify you that you're utilizing the right instrument for the errand:

v To split passwords, you require a splitting apparatus, for example, LC4, John the Ripper, or pwdump.

A general port scanner, for example, SuperScan, may not split passwords.

v For an inside and out investigation of a Web application, a Web-application survey meant apparatus, (for example, Whisker or WebInspect) is more fitting than a system analyzer, (for example, Ethereal).

At the point when selecting the right security instrument for the errand, make an inquiry or two. Get guidance from your associates and from other individuals on the web. A basic Group seek on Google (www.google.com) or scrutiny of security entrances, for example, SecurityFocus.com, SearchSecurity.com, and ITsecurity.com, frequently delivers extraordinary input from other security specialists.

Hundreds, if not thousands, of devices can be utilized for ethical hacking — from your own words and activities to programming based weakness appraisal star grams to equipment based system analyzers. The accompanying rundown keeps running down some of my most loved business, freeware, and open-source security devices:

vNmap

vEtherPeek

vSuperScan v QualysGuard v WebInspect

v LC4 (earlier called Lophtcrack)

vLANguard Network Security Scanner

v Network Stumbler

vToneLoc

Here are some other prominent apparatuses:

v Internet Scanner

v Ethereal v Nessus v Nikto

v Kismet

v THC-Scan

I examine these apparatuses and numerous others in Parts II through V when I go into the particular hack assaults. Index A contains a more far reaching posting of these devices for your reference.

The capacities of numerous security and hacking apparatuses are frequently misconstrued. This misconception has shed negative light on some fabulous devices, for example, SATAN (Security Administrator Tool for Analyzing Networks) and Nmap (Network Mapper).

Some of these devices are complex. Whichever apparatuses you utilize, acquaint yourself with them before you begin utilizing them. Here are approaches to do that:

v Read the readme and/or online help documents for your apparatuses.

v Study the client's aide for your business apparatuses.

v Consider formal classroom preparing from the security-apparatus seller or another outsider preparing supplier, if accessible.

Search for these attributes in apparatuses for ethical hacking:

v Adequate documentation.

v Detailed reports on the found vulnerabilities, including how they may be misused and altered.

v Updates and bolster when required.

v High-level reports that can be introduced to administrators or nontechie sorts. These elements can spare you time and exertion when you're composing the report.

Executing the arrangement

Ethical hacking can take constancy. Time and persistence are essential. Be cautious when you're performing your ethical hacking tests. A hacker in your system or an apparently generous representative looking behind you may watch what's going on. This individual could utilize this data against you.

It's not down to earth to verify that no hackers are on your frameworks before you begin. Simply verify you continue everything as calm and private as possible. This is particularly discriminating when transmitting and putting away your test outcomes. In the event that conceivable, encode these messages and documents utilizing Pretty Good Privacy (PGP) or something comparative. At any rate, watchword ensure them.

You're presently on a surveillance mission. Saddle however much data as could be expected about your association and frameworks, which is what vindictive hackers do. Begin with an expansive view and tight your core interest:

1.   Search the Internet for your association's name, your PC and system framework names, and your IP addresses.

Google is an awesome spot to begin for this.

2.   Narrow your degree, focusing on the particular frameworks you're testing.

Whether physical-security structures or Web applications, an easygoing evaluation can turn up much data about your frameworks.

3. Further tight your center with a more discriminating eye. Perform genuine outputs and other nitty gritty tests on your frameworks.

4. Perform the assaults, if that's what you decide to do.

Assessing results

Evaluate your outcomes to see what you uncovered, expecting that the vulnerabilities haven't been made evident before now. This is the place information tallies. Assessing the outcomes and connecting the particular vulnerabilities found is an ability that shows signs of improvement with experience. You'll wind up knowing your frameworks and also any other person. This makes the assessment handle much easier advancing.

Present a formal report to upper administration or to your client, laying out your outcomes. Keep these different gatherings on top of it to demonstrate that your endeavors and their cash are well spent. Section 17 depicts this procedure.

Proceeding onward

When you've completed your ethical hacking tests, regardless you have to actualize your investigation and proposals to verify your frameworks are secure.

New security vulnerabilities ceaselessly show up. Data frameworks constantly change and turn out to be more intricate. New hacker adventures and security vulnerabilities are frequently uncovered. You may find new ones! Security tests are a preview of the security stance of your frameworks. Whenever, everything can change, particularly after programming updates, including PC frameworks, or applying patches. Plan to test routinely (for instance, once every week or once per month

CHAPTER 8: PHYSICAL, DIGITAL, AND SOCIAL METHODS FOR ATTACKING

Physical security is a frequently neglected however discriminating part of a data security program. Your capacity to secure your data relies on upon your capacity to secure your site physically. In this part, I cover some regular physical security shortcomings as they identify with PCs and data security — you ought to pay special mind to these shortcomings in your frameworks. I likewise diagram free and ease countermeasures you can actualize to minimize your business' physical vulnerabilities.

I don't suggest breaking and entering, which would be important to test certain physical security vulnerabilities completely. Rather, approach those ranges to perceive how far you can get. Examine — from a pariah's viewpoint — at the physical vulnerabilities secured in this part. You may find openings in your physical security base that you had beforehand ignored.

Recognizing Basic Physical Security
Vulnerabilities

Whatever your PC and system security
innovation, essentially any hack is conceivable if
an attacker is in your building or server farm.
That's the reason searching for physical security
vulnerabilities and altering them before they're
misused is imperative.

In little organizations, some physical security
issues may not be an issue. Numerous physical
security vulnerabilities rely on upon such
variables as

- Size of the building

- Number of structures or destinations

- Number of workers

- Location and number of building passage and way out focuses

- Placement of the server farms and other private data

Actually a great many conceivable physical security vulnerabilities exist. The terrible fellows are dependably vigilant for them — so you ought to search for these vulnerabilities first. Here are a few illustrations of physical security vulnerabilities I've discovered when evaluating security for my customers:

- No secretary in a building to screen who's nearing and going

- No guest sign-in or escort needed for building access

- Employees trusting guests on the grounds that they wear merchant outfits or say they're in the building to take a shot at the copier or PCs

- No access controls on entryways or the utilization of conventional keys that can be copied with no responsibility

- Doors propped open

- IP-based feature, access control, and server farm administration frameworks available through the system with the default client ID and secret word
- Publicly open PC rooms
- Software and reinforcement media lying around

- Unsecured PC equipment, particularly portable PCs, telephones, and tablets

- Sensitive data being discarded in refuse jars as opposed to being destroyed or put in a shred compartment

- CDs and DVDs with secret data in rubbish jars

At the point when these physical security vulnerabilities are misused, awful things can happen. All it takes to abuse these shortcomings is an unapproved individual entering your building.

A Q&A on physical security with Jack Wiles

In this Q&A session, Jack Wiles, a data security pioneer with more than 30 years of experience, answers a few inquiries on physical security and how an absence of it frequently prompts information unreliability.

How imperative do you think physical security is in connection to specialized security issues?

JW: I've been posed that question ordinarily before, and from many years of involvement with both physical and specialized security, I have a standard answer. Without inquiry, a large number of the most lavish specialized security countermeasures and instruments regularly get to be useless when physical security is powerless. On the off chance that I can get my group into your building(s) and stroll up to somebody's work area and sign in as that individual, I have avoided all your specialized security frameworks. In past security evaluations, after my group and I entered a building, we generally found that individuals basically imagined that we had a place there — that we were representatives. We were constantly inviting and supportive when we interacted with genuine workers. They would regularly give back the graciousness by helping us with whatever we requested.

How were you ready to get into the vast majority of the structures when you directed "red group" penetration tests for organizations?

JW: In numerous cases, we just strongly strolled into the building and went up the lift in multistory structures. On the off chance that we were tested, we generally had a story prepared. Our commonplace story was that we felt that this was the HR leave ment, and we were there to seek work. In the event that we were ceased at the entryway and advised which building to go to for HR, we basically left and at that point searched for different doors to that same building. In the event that we discovered an outside smoking range at an alternate entryway, we endeavored tailgating and just strolled in behind different representatives who were returning the building after wrap up their breaks. Tailgating additionally worked at most passageways that obliged card access. In my vocation as a red-group pioneer, we were never ceased and addressed. We essentially said "thank you" as we strolled in and traded off the whole building.

What sorts of things would you bring out of a building?

JW: It was constantly simple to get enough essential documentation to demonstrate that we were there. As a rule, the documentation was sitting in a reuse box alongside somebody's work area (particularly if that individual was somebody essential). To us, that truly said, "Take me first!" We thought that it was fascinating that numerous organizations simply let their reuse boxes top off before exhausting them. We would likewise search for a room where strip-cut shredders were utilized. The reports that were destroyed were generally put away in clear plastic packs. We stacked these packs into our autos and had a large portion of the destroyed records set up back together in a couple of hours. We found that in the event that we glued the strips from any page on cardboard with as much as an inch of space between the strips, the last report was still discernable.

Jack Wiles is president of TheTrainingCo. (www.thetrainingco.com) and advances the yearly data security gathering Techno Security.

Pinpointing Physical Vulnerabilities in Your Office

Numerous potential physical security adventures appear to be improbable, however they can jump out at associations that don't consider physical security important. The awful gentlemen can abuse numerous physical security vulnerabilities, incorporating shortcomings in a building's base, office design, PC room get to, and plan. Notwithstanding these variables, consider the office's nearness to nearby crisis help (police, flame, and rescue vehicle) and the range's wrongdoing insights (bramble glary, breaking and entering, et cetera) so you can better comprehend what you're up against.

Search for the vulnerabilities examined in the accompanying segments when surveying your association's physical security. This won't take a considerable measure of specialized insightful or costly hardware. Contingent upon the extent of your offices, these tests shouldn't take much time either. What really matters is to figure out if the physical security controls are sufficient given what's in question. Most importantly, be functional and use the ability to think.

Building base

Entryways, windows, and dividers are basic segments of a building — particularly for a PC room or a range where classified data is put away.

Assault focuses

Hackers can misuse a modest bunch of building foundation vulnerabilities. Consider the accompanying ordinarily disregarded assault focuses:

✓ Are entryways propped open? Provided that this is true, why?

✓ Can holes at the base of discriminating entryways permit somebody utilizing an inflatable or other gadget to excursion a sensor within a "safe" room?

✓ Would it be anything but difficult to compel entryways open? A straightforward kick close to the doorknob is normally enough for standard entryways.

✓ What is the building or server farm made of (steel, wood, concrete), and how tough are the dividers and passages? How versatile is the material to tremors, tornadoes, solid winds, overwhelming downpours, and vehicles crashing into the building? Would these fiascos leave the building uncovered so that marauders and others with pernicious purpose could get entrance to the PC room or other discriminating ranges?

✓ Are any entryways or windows made of glass? Is this glass clear? Is the glass shatterproof or impenetrable?

✓ Do entryway relies on the outside make it simple for interlopers to unfasten them?

✓ Are entryways, windows, and other passage focuses wired to a caution framework?

✓ Are there drop roofs with tiles that can be pushed up? Are the dividers chunk to-piece? If not, somebody could undoubtedly scale dividers, bypassing any entryway or window access controls.

Countermeasures

Numerous physical security countermeasures for building vulnerabilities may require other support, development, or operations specialists. In the event that assembling framework is not your strength, you can employ outside specialists amid the outline, evaluation, and retrofitting stages to guarantee that you have sufficient controls. Here are a percentage of the most ideal approaches to set building security:

✓ Strong entryways and locks

✓   Windowless dividers around server farms

✓   A ceaselessly checked alert framework with system based cameras situated at all entrance focuses

✓   Lighting (particularly around passage and way out focuses)

✓   Mantraps and sallyports that permit stand out individual at once to go

CHAPTER 8: PHYSICAL, DIGITAL, AND SOCIAL METHODS FOR ATTACKING

Physical security is a frequently neglected however discriminating part of a data security program. Your capacity to secure your data relies on upon your capacity to secure your site physically. In this part, I cover some regular physical security shortcomings as they identify with PCs and data security — you ought to pay special mind to these shortcomings in your frameworks. I likewise diagram free and ease countermeasures you can actualize to minimize your business' physical vulnerabilities.

I don't suggest breaking and entering, which would be important to test certain physical security vulnerabilities completely. Rather, approach those ranges to perceive how far you can get. Examine — from a pariah's viewpoint — at the physical vulnerabilities secured in this part. You may find openings in your physical security base that you had beforehand ignored.

Recognizing Basic Physical Security Vulnerabilities

Whatever your PC and system security innovation, essentially any hack is conceivable if an attacker is in your building or server farm. That's the reason searching for physical security vulnerabilities and altering them before they're misused is imperative.

In little organizations, some physical security issues may not be an issue. Numerous physical security vulnerabilities rely on upon such variables as

- Size of the building

- Number of structures or destinations

- Number of workers

- Location and number of building passage and way out focuses

- Placement of the server farms and other private data

Actually a great many conceivable physical security vulnerabilities exist. The terrible fellows are dependably vigilant for them — so you ought to search for these vulnerabilities first. Here are a few illustrations of physical security vulnerabilities I've discovered when evaluating security for my customers:

- No secretary in a building to screen who's nearing and going

- No guest sign-in or escort needed for building access

- Employees trusting guests on the grounds that they wear merchant outfits or say they're in the building to take a shot at the copier or PCs

- No access controls on entryways or the utilization of conventional keys that can be copied with no responsibility

- Doors propped open

- IP-based feature, access control, and server farm administration frameworks available through the system with the default client ID and secret word
- Publicly open PC rooms
- Software and reinforcement media lying around

- Unsecured PC equipment, particularly portable PCs, telephones, and tablets

- Sensitive data being discarded in refuse jars as opposed to being destroyed or put in a shred compartment

- CDs and DVDs with secret data in rubbish jars

At the point when these physical security vulnerabilities are misused, awful things can happen. All it takes to abuse these shortcomings is an unapproved individual entering your building.

A Q&A on physical security with Jack Wiles

In this Q&A session, Jack Wiles, a data security pioneer with more than 30 years of experience, answers a few inquiries on physical security and how an absence of it frequently prompts information unreliability.

How imperative do you think physical security is in connection to specialized security issues?

JW: I've been posed that question ordinarily before, and from many years of involvement with both physical and specialized security, I have a standard answer. Without inquiry, a large number of the most lavish specialized security countermeasures and instruments regularly get to be useless when physical security is powerless. On the off chance that I can get my group into your building(s) and stroll up to somebody's work area and sign in as that individual, I have avoided all your specialized security frameworks. In past security evaluations, after my group and I entered a building, we generally found that individuals basically imagined that we had a place there — that we were representatives. We were constantly inviting and supportive when we interacted with genuine workers. They would regularly give back the graciousness by helping us with whatever we requested.

How were you ready to get into the vast majority of the structures when you directed "red group" penetration tests for organizations?

JW: In numerous cases, we just strongly strolled into the building and went up the lift in multistory structures. On the off chance that we were tested, we generally had a story prepared. Our commonplace story was that we felt that this was the HR leave ment, and we were there to seek work. In the event that we were ceased at the entryway and advised which building to go to for HR, we basically left and at that point searched for different doors to that same building. In the event that we discovered an outside smoking range at an alternate entryway, we endeavored tailgating and just strolled in behind different representatives who were returning the building after wrap up their breaks. Tailgating additionally worked at most passageways that obliged card access. In my vocation as a red-group pioneer, we were never ceased and addressed. We essentially said "thank you" as we strolled in and traded off the whole building.

What sorts of things would you bring out of a building?

JW: It was constantly simple to get enough essential documentation to demonstrate that we were there. As a rule, the documentation was sitting in a reuse box alongside somebody's work area (particularly if that individual was somebody essential). To us, that truly said, "Take me first!" We thought that it was fascinating that numerous organizations simply let their reuse boxes top off before exhausting them. We would likewise search for a room where strip-cut shredders were utilized. The reports that were destroyed were generally put away in clear plastic packs. We stacked these packs into our autos and had a large portion of the destroyed records set up back together in a couple of hours. We found that in the event that we glued the strips from any page on cardboard with as much as an inch of space between the strips, the last report was still discernable.

Jack Wiles is president of TheTrainingCo. (www.thetrainingco.com) and advances the yearly data security gathering Techno Security.

Pinpointing Physical Vulnerabilities in Your Office

Numerous potential physical security adventures appear to be improbable, however they can jump out at associations that don't consider physical security important. The awful gentlemen can abuse numerous physical security vulnerabilities, incorporating shortcomings in a building's base, office design, PC room get to, and plan.

Notwithstanding these variables, consider the office's nearness to nearby crisis help (police, flame, and rescue vehicle) and the range's wrongdoing insights (bramble glary, breaking and entering, et cetera) so you can better comprehend what you're up against.

Search for the vulnerabilities examined in the accompanying segments when surveying your association's physical security. This won't take a considerable measure of specialized insightful or costly hardware. Contingent upon the extent of your offices, these tests shouldn't take much time either. What really matters is to figure out if the physical security controls are sufficient given what's in question. Most importantly, be functional and use the ability to think.

Building base

Entryways, windows, and dividers are basic segments of a building — particularly for a PC

room or a range where classified data is put
away.

Assault focuses

Hackers can misuse a modest bunch of building
foundation vulnerabilities. Consider the
accompanying ordinarily disregarded assault
focuses:

✓   Are entryways propped open? Provided
that this is true, why?

✓   Can holes at the base of discriminating
entryways permit somebody utilizing an
inflatable or other gadget to excursion a sensor
within a "safe" room?

✓   Would it be anything but difficult to
compel entryways open? A straightforward kick

close to the doorknob is normally enough for standard entryways.

✓   What is the building or server farm made of (steel, wood, concrete), and how tough are the dividers and passages? How versatile is the material to tremors, tornadoes, solid winds, overwhelming downpours, and vehicles crashing into the building? Would these fiascos leave the building uncovered so that marauders and others with pernicious purpose could get entrance to the PC room or other discriminating ranges?

✓   Are any entryways or windows made of glass? Is this glass clear? Is the glass shatterproof or impenetrable?

✓   Do entryway relies on the outside make it simple for interlopers to unfasten them?

✓   Are entryways, windows, and other passage focuses wired to a caution framework?

✓   Are there drop roofs with tiles that can be pushed up? Are the dividers chunk to-piece? If not, somebody could undoubtedly scale dividers, bypassing any entryway or window access controls.

Countermeasures

Numerous physical security countermeasures for building vulnerabilities may require other support, development, or operations specialists. In the event that assembling framework is not your strength, you can employ outside specialists amid the outline, evaluation, and retrofitting stages to guarantee that you have sufficient controls. Here are a percentage of the most ideal approaches to set building security:

✓   Strong entryways and locks

✓   Windowless dividers around server farms

✓   A ceaselessly checked alert framework with system based cameras situated at all entrance focuses

✓   Lighting (particularly around passage and way out focuses)

✓   Mantraps and sallyports that permit stand out individual at once to go

CHAPTER 10: NETWORK INFRASTRUCTURE VULNERABILITIES

A PC system is an accumulation of gadgets that can impart together through characterized pathways. It is as it were the fabric that ties business applications together. It runs from shared, individual region systems (PANs), neighborhood (LANs), grounds zone systems (CANs), stockpiling territory systems (SANs), metropolitan range systems (MANs) and wide region net-works (WANs). Now and then, there is the requirement for web integration to encourage wide scope zone reach. A practical PC system can fundamentally be made out of PCs, system interface cards, servers, switches, switches, links, conventions, applications etc.

Normal topologies used to actualize system associations incorporate ring, transport star, cross section, and half breed. In any case, star is the most broadly utilized topology because of its adaptability, effectiveness and robustness. The medium of correspondence may be in light of wired or remote advances and can be required by changing elements.

Vulnerabilities in Network Infrastructures

What's more, an internetwork can be made by associating two or more LANs or WANs. Applications that keep running on these systems incorporate messages, moment delivery people, internet amusements, web programs, record exchange convention and database applications to say yet a couple. Transmission of information follows an arrangement of guidelines and rules endorsed by the Open Systems Interconnection (OSI) Model which comprises of seven layers to be specific – application, presentation, session, transport, system, information connection and physical layers.

System Vulnerabilities

Pernicious clients are dependably sneaking around to sneak into systems and make issues and consequently, they antagonistically influence a few organizations around the globe overall. In 2002, the CSI/FBI Computer Crime Security Survey noticed that 90 percent of respondents recognized security breaks, yet just 34 percent reported the criminal acts to law implementation offices (Knapp &Boulton, 2006). This goes to demonstrate that no framework is totally insusceptible from such potential security ruptures.

When all is said in done terms, framework helplessness is a defect or shortcoming in the outline or usage of a data framework (counting the security methods and security controls connected with the framework) that could be purposefully or unexpectedly misused to antagonistically influence an organization's operations or resources through a loss of privacy, trustworthiness or accessibility (NIST, 2010).

What then is system powerlessness? As plain as this may appear, this idea is very much an uneasy term to characterize. At first glance, system defenselessness is anything that represents a potential parkway for assault or security break against a framework. This can incorporate things like infections, passwords composed on sticky cushions, mistakenly designed frameworks et cetera. This kind of indecencies expand the danger to a framework, however there is a more extensive connection to this idea than have been expressed above and also inside of the security group.

In perspective of the prior and in the connection important to security experts, system vulnerability is a security presentation that has the penchant to bring about a surprising and undesirable occasion that bargains the security of a system base as an aftereffect of the presence of a feeble ness, outline, or execution mistake. In other words, system defenselessness is a blemish inside of a sys-tem that makes it incomprehensible even where usage and organization is legitimately done, to keep an interloper from unapproved access to a system and an ensuing modification operation and information bargain on it; or the illicit usurping of trust. By and large, particularly where the defenselessness is programming focused, it is normal that such found imperfections are settled by the vendor through the arrival of patches.

The requirement for secure system has and will dependably be of foremost significance to anybody outlining or overseeing it. The security of any system includes the prosperity of data and base in which the likelihood of fruitful yet undetected burglary, altering, and disruption of data and administrations is kept low or mediocre (Kuhn, Walsh & Fries, 2005). A security system is one that brags of a satisfactory uprightness (dependability of information and system re-sources), credibility (acknowledgment and surety of the data root), accessibility (condition whereby coveted assets are open and possible) and secrecy (protection of in-arrangement or assets). It is regularly said that if a hacker needs to get inside your framework or system as the case may be, there is nothing you can do about it. Maybe, what should be possible is to fumes all roads at making it to a great degree harder for the hacker to rupture the framework's security.

Some system/framework vulnerabilities incorporate (yet not constrained to) the accompanying:

1. Unstable/uncovered Ports.
2. Unpredictable empowering of administrations.
3. Despicable framework setup
4. Poor hostile to infection execution.
5. Poor firewall sending.
6. Poor interruption discovery framework (IDS) setups.
7. Week watchword execution.
8. Simple access to data.

9. Downloading of records and applications from locales that are not trusted.

10. Unsecure applications/programs as a consequence of poor programming practices.

11. Application secondary passages.

12. Absence of fitting security strategies.

13. Not offering thoughtfulness regarding security pointers – clients neglect to give legitimate consideration by declining to peruse the notice messages or security markers.

14. Disappointed representatives.

15. Absence of proficient physical security.

16. Deficient security preparing and mindfulness.

17. Heedlessness on the way of clients.

Corporate Espionage.

The causative elements recorded above can be abridged into two classifications:

1. Application/programming vulnerabilities
2. Human related vulnerabilities – clients being powerless connections through which breaks can be made to the security of systems/frameworks.

A few Modes of Attack

1. Hacking: this is the unapproved getting to of a PC framework for information or data fitting in with another person. The hacker does this by abusing an objective frameworks' shortcoming or defenselessness. A hacker can utilize the procedures of both infections and worms, on the other hand, the hacker may dodge IDS (Intrusion Detection System) discovery by keenly masking the assault. Kevin Mitnick, remarkable for his hacking adventures, generally utilized social building procedures to break into frameworks (Newson, 2005). In perspective of the prior, there are different channels through which a hacker can obtain entrance to a framework. These include:

a. Application-level assaults: this is on the grounds that today, programming engineers are most times under weight to convey items in great time combined with the increment popular for amazing programming inside of programming building approach. The mind boggling arrangements being illuminated today have offered ascent to tremendous measures of components and functionalities in what applications convey. Everything these needs at times set aside a few minutes of the substance and in light of the fact that this element is not generally adequate, aggregate and definitive testing is barely fulfilled before the item is discharged. Most times usage of security instruments turn into an untimely idea and are conveyed as "extra" segments. Cushion Overflow Attacks can be utilized to break such inadequately secure applications because of poor or non-exhibit blunder checking components (Berg, 2007).

b. Misconfiguration assaults: hackers get a field day around despicably designed sys-tem as an aftereffect of amateurish administration of such frameworks. Because of the complexities of frameworks today, managers who are not extremely gifted are found napping by prowling hackers.

c. Working frameworks assault: because of the complexities of today's systems, working systems run numerous administrations, ports and methods of access and would take a horrendous part to keep a potential security break. Incredible arrangements of administrations are continued running moreover open ports when the default settings of working frameworks are actualized amid in-

Vulnerabilities in Network Infrastructures installation. Subsequently, to increase unapproved access to network frameworks, hackers search for and adventure working framework vulnerabilities (Chen & Davis, 2006)).

2. SQL infusion: this is a kind of security adventure whereby the attacker infuses Structured Query Language (SQL) code through a web structure data box, to obtain entrance to assets, or roll out improvements to information. Here, the attacker infuses SQL summons to misuse non-accepted info vulnerabilities in a web application database backend and hence execute self-assertive SQL charges through the web application. Since developers use consecutive orders with client data, it makes it simpler for attackers to infuse charges. (Dahse, 2010)

3. Secret word breaking: Password splitting is a term used to portray the penetration of a system, framework, or asset with or without the utilization of apparatuses to open an asset that has been secured with a watchword. Watchword splitting doesn't generally include advanced instruments. It can be as straightforward as discovering a sticky note with the secret word composed on it adhered right to the screen or covered up under a console. Another unrefined strategy is known as "dumpster plunging," which essentially includes an attacker experiencing waste to discover disposed of documentation that may contain passwords. Obviously, assaults can include far more noteworthy levels of complexity and this incorporates the utilization of methods, for example, beast power, word reference and crossover assaults. There exists the likelihood for secret word wafers to identify encoded passwords, recover such from a PC's memory and afterward unscramble it. The point of a secret word wafer is basically to acquire the root/executive watchword of the objective framework; this is on account of the director right gives the attacker access to records and applications and can introduce a secondary passage, for example, a Trojan, for future access to the framework. The attacker can likewise introduce a system sniffer to sniff the inner system activity with the goal that he will have the greater part of the data went around the system. Subsequent to picking up root air conditioning cess, the attacker heightens the benefits to that of the overseer. More often than not, the attacker utilizes a framework that has a more prominent figuring force than that of the objective for proficient splitting of the watchword (Shimonski, 2002).

4. **Phishing:** this is a method for endeavoring to obtain data, for example, usernames, passwords and charge card points of interest by taking on the appearance of a dependable substance in an electronic correspondence. Interchanges indicating to be from well known

social sites, closeout locales, online installment processors or IT managers are normally used to draw the un-suspecting open and thusly a client is persuaded to dole out significant information. This is further accomplished by diverting the client to an alternate site through messages, texts and so on. Phishers offer illegitimate sites to the client to fill individual in-development. The fundamental motivation behind phishing is to become acquainted with the client's ledgers, passwords and other security data. Attackers can get the crowd through mass-mailing a great many email addresses far and wide. Phishers can trick clients by convincing them to get into a fake site with the area name marginally not quite the same as the first site which is hard to take note. They utilize the pictures of the genuine hyper-join, which itself causes as a hyperlink to an unapproved site. At times, Phishers additionally misuse SMTP (Simple Mail Transfer Protocol) defects. By and large, phishing includes enlisting a fake space name, assembling a clone site and afterward sending messages to numerous clients (Tan, 2006).

5. Social designing: this is the human side of breaking into a corporate system. Companies with verification forms, firewalls, virtual private systems (VPNs) and net-work observing programming are still open to assaults. A representative may unwittingly dole out key data on an email or by noting inquiries via telephone with somebody they don't have the foggiest idea, or even by discussing a task with colleagues at a neighborhood after work hours. It is the tactic or trick of gaining sensitive information by exploiting the basic human nature such as: trust, fear and the desire to help. Social engineers try to gather information such as: sensitive information, authorization and access details. Social engineering is the hardest form of attack to defend against because it cannot be defended with hardware or software alone and because people are the weakest link in the security chain, a successful defense will be to have good policies and the education of employees to follow such (Peltier, 2006). Eavesdropping, shoulder surfing, dumpster diving (search-ing waste/trash bins for valuable information), tailgating, piggybacking etc. are all ways through which social engineers carry out their activities.

6. Sniffers: this is a program or device that captures the vital information from the network traffic specific to a particular network. Sniffing is basically a data interception policy whose objective is to steal passwords (from email, the web, FTP, SQL or telnet), email text, files in transfer etc. Protocols vulnerable to sniffing include telnet, HTTP, FTP, POP, NNTP, SMTP and IMAP. Sniffing can be passive (sniffing through a hub, this is difficult to detect) or active (sniffing through a switch). (Gandhi & Srivatsa, 2010).

7. Viruses and worms: a virus is a self-replicating malicious program that replicates its own code by attaching copies of itself into other executable codes and operates without the knowledge of the computer user posing serious threat to both business and personnel. It resides in the memory and replicates itself while the program where it is attached is running. It can transform itself by changing codes to appear different. Viruses hide them-selves from detection by encrypting themselves into the cryptic symbols, altering the disk directory data to compensate the additional virus bytes or using stealth algorithms to redirect disk data. Worms on the other hand are distinguished from viruses by the fact that a virus requires some form of human intervention to infect a computer whereas a worm does not. A worm can also be said to be a special type of virus that has the ability to replicate itself and use memory, but cannot attach itself to other programs. A worm spreads through the infected network automatically but a virus does not. Some indications of virus threat include:

    a) Programs take longer to load than normal

b) Computer's hard drive constantly run out of disk space

c) Files have strange names which are not recognizable

d) Programs act erratically

e) Resources are used up easily.

8. Trojan: this is a malicious application that is unable to spread of its own accord. Historically, the term has been used to refer to applications that appear legitimate and useful, but perform malicious and illicit activities on an affected computer. Trojan types include security software disablers, data-sending Trojans, remote access Trojans, destructive Trojans, proxy Trojans, FTP Trojans, denial-of-service Trojans. In general, Trojans can gain access into a system through physical access, instant messenger applications, attachments, browser and email software bugs, fake programs, untrusted sites and freeware software, downloading files, games and screensavers from the internet, legitimate shrink-wrapped software package by a disgruntled employee etc. Most times they reside deep in the system and make registry changes that allow it to meet its purpose as a remote administration tool. With the Trojan, a whole lot of protocols and ports come under severe attacks. Popular Trojans include back orifice and netbus (Microsoft Malware Protection Centre, 2011). Some manifestations of Trojan attack include:

Vulnerabilities in Network Infrastructures

a. CD-ROM drive opens and closes by itself.
b. Computer screen flips upside down or inverts.
c. Wallpaper or background settings change by themselves.
d. Documents or messages print from the printer themselves.
e. Screensaver settings change by themselves.
f. Computer browser goes to a strange or unknown web page by itself.

g. Windows color settings change by themselves.

h. Right and left mouse buttons reverse their functions.

i. Windows start button disappears.

j. Mouse pointer disappears.

k. Mouse pointer moves and functions by itself.

l. Strange chat boxes appear on the victim's computer.

m. The ISP complains to the victim that his/her computer is IP scanning.

9. Spamming: this involves populating the inbox of a target group with junk or unsolicited emails. Spammers get access to the email ID's when the user registers to any email ser-vice, forum, or blogs by hacking the information, or registers as genuine users. Spam emails sometimes contain malicious computer programs such as viruses and Trojans which cause change in the computer system or serves as a tracking tool on the system. Some techniques used to effect spamming include spoofing the domain, social engineer-ing, directory harvesting, phishing, sending virus attached files, database poisoning etc. however, spamming has legitimate use as is the case in advertising (Bradley, 2009).

10. Buffer overflows: this takes place when a buffer that has been assigned a specified storage space, has more data passed on to it than it can accommodate. As a way of exploiting buffer overflow to gain access in order to gain or escalate privileges, the offender creates the data to be fed to the application; this is because random data will generate a segmentation fault or bus error, never a remote shell or the execution of a command (Kramer David, 2001).

In July 2000, a vulnerability to buffer overflow attack was discovered in Microsoft Out-look and Outlook Express. A programming flaw made it possible for an attacker to com-promise the integrity of the target computer by simply sending an e-mail message. Unlike the typical email virus, users could not protect themselves by not opening attached files; in fact, the user did not even have to open the message to enable the attack. The pro-grams' message header mechanisms had a defect that made it possible for senders to overflow the area with extraneous data, which allowed them to execute whatever type of code they desired on the recipient's computers. Because the process was activated as soon as the recipient downloaded the message from the server, this type of buffer overflow attack is very difficult to defend. Microsoft has since created a patch to eliminate the vulnerability (Kramer David, 2001).

Prevention/Containment Measures

Vulnerabilities can be successfully contained when certain measures are put in place such as ask-ing the right questions and anticipating every step and potential threat. Such questions include ascertaining what the intruder can see on a target system, what the intruder can do with the information and if there are ways of substantiating the footprints after a potential breach. The ability to substantiate a security breach becomes handy for legal measures. It is incumbent on any network administrator to be adept with the design weaknesses that exposes an operating system and its corresponding applications to attack hence; a thorough understanding of products and technologies is paramount. Also, he gathers information about viruses and worms, identifies and correct network vulnerabilities, gets information that helps to prevent security problems and in the event of an eventual successful attack – a way to recover from such, in good time.

1. To avoid SQL infusion,
    a. Decrease the benefits of database associations.
    b. Incapacitate verbose mistake messages.
    c. Shield the framework account.
    d. Review the source codes

e. Never trust client enter rather, affirm by method for validation, all textbox sections utilizing acceptance controls, general expressions, code etc.

f. Never utilize dynamic SQL rather, utilize parameterized SQL or put away systems.

g. Never join with a database utilizing an administrator level record rather, utilize a restricted access record to unite with the database.

2. To counteract secret word breaking:

a. Pick passwords that have at the very least eight characters.

b. Passwords ought to have a blend of lower and upper case letters, numbers, special characters and so on. This makes it hard to break.

c. Try not to utilize words that can be effectively found in the lexicon as passwords.

d. Try not to utilize open data, for example, standardized savings number, MasterCard number and ATM card number as passwords.

e. Never utilize individual data as passwords.

f. Usernames and passwords ought to appear as something else.

g. Administrators and overseers can upgrade the security of their systems by setting solid passwords arrangements. This can be further improved by guaranteeing that secret key prerequisites are incorporated with authoritative security strategies.

h. At the point when putting in new frameworks, verify default passwords are promptly changed. (Shimonski, 2002).

3. One great method for forestalling phishing, is through the organization of hostile to phishing delicate product. This product is known not phishing assaults inside of the site or in the customer's email. The product shows the genuine site area that the client is going by dwelling at the web programs and email servers, as a fundamental apparatus. It is critical that phishing assaults can be averted at the server side furthermore the customer side. Examples of these apparatuses include: PhishTank Site Checker, Nercraft, GFI MailEssentials and SpoofGuard.

4. To counteract or reduce social designing as a method of assault is unwieldy. This is be-cause it is extremely hard to identify since there is no technique that guarantees complete security from a potential assault. There is no particular programming or equipment for protecting

against a social building assault. However this threat can be minimized through:

a. Trainings which ought to comprise of all security approaches routines to expand mindfulness on social designing.

b. Secret word arrangements: there ought to be intermittent change in passwords, utilization of extensive and complex passwords.

c. Guaranteeing the security of touchy data and approved utilization of assets.

d. Physical security approaches, for example, ID of workers utilizing biometrics, escorting of guests, range confinements and peaceful areas (DMZs), fitting shred-ding of futile reports and utilizing security faculty.

e. Data ought to be characterized into classifications, for example, top mystery, exclusive, for internal utilize just, for open utilize, etc.

5. To anticipate/contain the overabundances of sniffers:

   a. Check which machines are running in indiscriminate mode.

   b. Limitation of physical access to network media guarantees that a bundle sniffer can't be introduced.

   c. Encryption: this is the best security measure against sniffers. It would not keep a sniffer from working but rather will guarantee that what a sniffer peruses is not critical.

   d. Apply the most recent patches or other lockdown methods to the framework.

   e. For all time include the MAC location of the door to the ARP reserve.

   f. Change the convention used to encourage remote login from telnet to SSH.

g. For little systems, use static IP locations and static ARP tables while for substantial net-works, empower port security highlights.

h. Send hostile to sniffing instruments, for example, ARP Watch and Prodetect.

6. Infections and worms are to a great extent put on check by the establishment of cutting-edge hostile to infection virtual products that sweep the framework routinely at planned times. Respectability checking and between caption are different infection recognition systems.

7. To identify Trojans:

a. Routinely check for flawed system exercises utilizing devices like Ethereal.

b. Routinely check for flawed registry passages utilizing apparatuses, for example, MS Config.

c. Routinely check for flawed open ports utilizing devices, for example, Netstat, Fport and TCPView.

d. Routinely run Trojan scanner to recognize Trojans.

e. Routinely check for running procedures.

f. Erase suspicious and unaccountable gadget drivers.

g. Introduce hostile to Trojan programming projects.

8. To contain spamming, hostile to spam instruments, for example, AEVITA and Spam Bully ought to be in-slowed down.

9. To counteract cradle floods:

a. Execute manual reviewing of codes.

b. Debilitate stack execution.

c. Execute more secure C library support.

d. Receive productive and hearty methods.

Different measures include:

1. Patch administration: this is the procedure of guaranteeing that suitable patches are in-slowed down on a framework. It includes:

  a. Picking, confirming, testing and applying patches.
  b. Redesigning already connected patches with current patches.
  c. Posting patches connected already to the present programming.
  d. Recording stores or warehouses of patches for simple choice.
  e. Allotting and sending connected patches. (Mell, Bergeron & Henning, 2005)

2. Security union: this is the procedure of reusing and mixing different technologies to make better than ever capacities and items. This incorporates mix of security capacities and data into a typical IP system. This measure can influence innovation to enhance the execution of the security capacity both physically and consistently. Summarily, it is a three-pronged methodology made out of technologies, security procedures and individuals (EC-Council).

3. Firewall innovations: these are projects or equipment gadgets that secure the re-wellsprings of a private system from clients of different systems. Firewalls are in charge of approaching activity to be permitted to pass, square or reject and they likewise work with intermediary servers. They help in the security of private systems from interlopers (EC-Council).

4. Making security strategies: security arrangements are reports that depict the security controls that will be executed in an organization at an abnormal state without which the organization can't be shielded from conceivable claims, lost income, awful reputation and essential security assaults. These arrangements set the destinations and tenets of conduct for users and directors furthermore propose the security measures to be followed in an organization. Approaches accomplish three objectives, specifically:

a. They lessen or kill lawful obligation to representatives and outsiders.

b. They ensure secret, restrictive data from robbery, abuse, unauthorized exposure or alteration.

c. They counteract misuse of organization registering assets (EC-Council).

5. Penetration testing: this is a system used to survey the security model of an organization all in all, and thusly uncovering conceivable results of a genuine attacker rupturing the system security. At the point when this test is not adequately and professionally completed, it can bring about the loss of administrations and interruption of business exercises and in addition congruity.

6. Physical security: this portrays the systems put set up to secure faculty, basic resources and frameworks against purposeful and unintentional dangers. This is to pre-vent unapproved access to PC frameworks, anticipate stealing and altering of da-ta from PC frameworks, keep the loss of information/harm to frameworks against any characteristic catastrophe or fire episode and ensure the dependability of the information put away in the PC. These measures can be:

a. Physical – to secure resources e.g. sending security work force.
b. Specialized – to secure administrations and components that bolster data innovation e.g. security for server rooms and extravagant gadgetry.
c. Operational – measures taken before performing an operation, for example, investigating dangers of an action and taking fitting countermeasures.

7. Cryptography – this is the study of encoding content in configurations that are difficult to get it. Plain messages are scrambled into disjointed configurations called figure content which is in light of numerical calculations that utilization mystery keys for secure change back to clear content. (Barr, 2001)

8. Interruption Detection Systems (IDSs):

These are systems that are utilized to screen system movement, check for suspicious exercises and advise the system executive or the framework. In a few occurrences, the IDS may additionally respond to noxious or bizarre activity and will make a move, for example, notwithstanding the client or maybe the IP location source from getting to the framework. (http://www.intrusiondetectionsystem.org)

Evaluating Network Vulnerabilities

A legitimately executed system security assessment includes three fundamental stages. These stages are:

1. Arranging – in this stage, an official understanding is marked between concerned gatherings. This archive is intended to contain both lawful and non-revelation conditions that

serve to secure the ethical hacker against conceivable claim amid this stage.

2. Conduct – this stage includes the assessment of specialized reports arranged taking into account test-ing potential vulnerabilities.

3. Surmising – in this stage, the consequences of the assessment are conveyed to the organization or backers and remedial move is made if necessary.

Ways to deal with proactively secure a system and keep outlandish interruption from dangerous components include:

Vulnerabilities in Network Infrastructures

1. Endeavoring to reproduce oneself as a gatecrasher attempting to assault ones system from a remote area through the web.

2. Endeavoring to mimic oneself as an interloper attempting to assault ones system by propelling assaults against the customer's modem pools.

3. Testing inside of a nearby system to check whether a client inside of the system has the capacity pick up unauthorized access to another area on the system.

4. Endeavoring to take critical information or data asset from a worker to determine the level of mindfulness that individuals from staff have toward social designing as a danger to framework security.

5. Endeavoring to physically trade off the ICT framework of the association to dissuade mine the level and effectiveness of physical security.

Any Network Vulnerability Assessment activity comprises of the accompanying steps:

1. Discovering all the hosts on the system.

2. Fingerprinting their Operating frameworks.

3. Distinguishing open ports on the framework.

4. Mapping the ports to different system administrations.

5. Distinguishing the rendition of the administrations running.

6. Mapping the administration form to different found security vulnerabilities.

7. Confirming if the administration on the host is really powerless against an assault or on the off chance that it has been fixed.

Burdens/Effects on Business

1. Loss of believability and trust of clients

2. Loss of protection and harm to goodwill

3. As per specialists, organizations most at danger are those taking care of online money related transactions.

4. Financial misfortune

5. Interim or perpetual conclusion

6. Introduction to wanton claims and discretions

7. Standing out as truly newsworthy for all the reasons

CHAPTER 11: WIRELESS LAN VULNERABILITIES

A sweep of today's system commercial center demonstrates that remote systems administration is prepared for arrangement in organizations, even in inclination to the wired systems that are presently ordinary. The capacity to introduce a neighborhood (LAN) and to move system stations without the expense of introducing or changing cabling in effectively assembled offices is a noteworthy advantage of this innovation. Since the mid-1990s, the specialized measures hidden these systems have advanced from different restrictive details into a couple by and large settled upon global guidelines. This, thusly, has given the capacity to develop systems contained items from more than a solitary merchant. System velocities have ascended from a couple of hundred kilobits for each second to no less than 10 megabits for every second, rates that are completely aggressive with wired 10BaseT Ethernet systems. This has made the versatile utilization of remote systems conceivable as well as plausible, and they can be found in numerous air terminal clubs, lodgings, office structures and even Starbucks espresso shops.1, 2 To make things significantly more alluring, costs have fallen and almost 20 percent of organizations studied by Sage Research now have introduced remote networks.3

Remote LANs, nonetheless, still have their issues. Associating system components by radio waves rather than wires presents numerous difficulties. From the dependability point of view, it is hard to foresee from the earlier the reliable scope of a remote system radio inside a building. This is generally in light of the fact that building development differs broadly, and things like steel bars and vigorously put dividers extremely weaken radio waves. Notwithstanding for outside structures, foreseeing scope is troublesome because of radio engendering issues, for example, multipath blurring, which are probabilistic and not deterministic. Maybe additionally alarming is that, by their extremely nature, remote LANs telecast information into space, where they can be blocked by anybody with the capacity to listen in at the suitable recurrence. More regrettable, the very elements that encourage vagrant utilization of remote LANs additionally empower intruders to effortlessly enter such systems unless measures are taken to relieve those threats.4 That exhibits a noteworthy security hazard. What's more, despite the fact that speeds are similar to 10BaseT Ethernets, regardless they are much slower than 100BaseT Fast Ethernet.

This section gives a review of how remote LANs work, while inspecting the dangers, vulnerabilities and dangers that influence remote systems uniquely in contrast to their wired brethren.

Remote LAN Technology

At root, every single remote Lan are radio systems. The signs going among the system stations are high-recurrence motions in the scope of 10 MHz to 300 MHz or higher. What recognizes remote LANs from their wired family is that wired systems endeavor to keep these signs to links and perspective sign spread from the system links as an issue. Remote systems intentionally telecast their information as radio waves, and after that get them out of the air to finish the system association. Likewise with diversion radio and TV, it is not functional to telecast the system spine flags straightforwardly, so a procedure known as balance inspires them onto another radio recurrence - the transporter.

The sorts of tweak utilized for remote LANs fall into the class known as spread range. Spread range signs possess a substantial segment of the appointed radio range, instead of being barely fixated on the transporter recurrence, as is standard with radio and TV slots. Military applications drove the advancement of spread range innovation. One point of interest of spread range is that it is tolerant of obstruction from restricted band signals (as are radio and TV slots) than are tight band regulation procedures. This favorable position is accomplished at the expense of expanded intricacy. Luckily, present day extensive scale joining (LSI) innovation makes it conceivable to understand a handy and reasonable spread range framework on only a couple, or even a solitary, coordinated circuit.

There are two essential sorts of spread range regulation utilized for remote LANs:5

Recurrence bouncing spread range (FHSS) is a framework wherein the transmitter always shows signs of change recurrence inside of an appointed extent, staying just a brief while on every recurrence went to. Plainly, the transmitter and recipient must move frequencies (jump) in step, which obliges that they share a key containing the bounce arrangement. US Federal Communications Commission (FCC) standards oblige that, in the most-utilized groups, the jump grouping utilizing channels separated at 1 MHz interims must cover no less than 75 directs in the allocated band and not stay on any single channel for more than 400 milliseconds in any 30-second period.6

Direct succession spread range (DSSS) accomplishes the spreading of the sign by regulating the information with a key arrangement known as the chipping code. The consequence of this operation is a sign spread over the coveted recurrence band, as is accomplished with FHSS. DSSS by and large can bolster higher information rates than FHSS, and is more tolerant of most sorts of impedance. Like FHSS, it obliges that transmitter and recipient share a mystery, for this situation, the chipping code.

It is imperative to note that remote systems, as an immediate consequence of the sort of balance they utilize, are private key frameworks. All stations on a given system share a typical key.

This encourages administration, yet causes security issues.

Another sort of adjustment, orthogonal recurrence division multiplexing (OFDM), is anticipated utilization when rapid remote LANs get to be accessible. Generally, OFDM includes part the info information into a few parallel streams, tweaking every stream onto a different transporter recurrence, then demodulating all the transporters at the far off end and recombining the information into a copy of the first.

Remote LANs accessible and arranged as of now work in one of three radio groups assigned as modern, experimental and medicinal (ISM). These groups are situated at 900 MHz (902-928 MHz), 2.4 GHz (2400-2483.5 MHz) and 5.8 GHz (5725-5850 MHz).7 Devices that additionally work in these groups are microwave stoves (in the 2.4 GHz band) and cordless phones (in both the 900 MHz and 2.4 GHz groups). The 5.8 GHz band is not yet in wide utilize, but rather that in all likelihood will change before long.8 The fascination of the ISM groups is that under Part 15 of the FCC Rules, the gear administrator obliges no permit to work radio hardware at those frequencies.9 The main prerequisite is that the gear has been ensured by the maker to the authorizing power (an administration office) as meeting the specialized prerequisites built up by the organization for operation inside of the ISM band. Those prerequisites incorporate determining balance sort, force yield and certification that the gadget does not put the administrator at danger.

This fascination has a monstrous side, in any case. Gear that works under the Part 15 FCC Rules must share this range on an apathy premise with authorized clients in the same band.10 Simply put, remote LANs should not bring about impedance to authorized clients in the ISM recurrence band, and must acknowledge any obstruction they experience. This is a critical configuration and operational test, and it is a demonstration of the condition of current innovation that these frameworks work by any means, significantly less at high information rates in basic applications.

A late option is the expansion of an Unlicensed National Information Infrastructure (UNII) 5GHz band, which underpins high information rates and guarantees less impedance than the ISM groups.

Like cordless phones, remote LANs are utilized basically as augmentations of settled systems. They are joined with the altered system by an entrance point, which works as an extension between the settled and remote bits of the system. Albeit remote LANs are fundamentally Ethernets, another convention suite is obliged to guarantee interoperability. Table 1 demonstrates the dominating remote LAN models. The Institute of Electrical and Electronics Engineers (IEEE) has distributed a draft standard, IEEE 802.11e. Its design is to include nature of administration particulars and keep up in reverse similarity with the prior 802.11 variations. This is proposed to determine a noteworthy inadequacy with the current 802.11 family, in particular the absence of nature of-administration standards.11 It is still in the remark stage.

The other major WLAN guidelines issue is the perpetual North America/European Union challenge. The current measures for WLANs inside of the European group are HiperLAN and HiperLAN/2, abridged in table 1. It can be contended that the HiperLAN standard is in fact better than 802.11, yet the 802.11 family piece of the pie keeps on growing, potentially inferable from the 5 to 15 percent value premium for HiperLAN/2. The IEEE has presented another variation of 802.11a, named 802.11h, which includes transmit force control (TPC) and element recurrence choice (DFS) to the 802.11a standard to manage specific impedance issues found in Europe, where the 5 GHz band is imparted to guard foundation and NATO radars and satellites.12 At slightest one merchant, Philips, has chosen that the future lies with the 802.11h standard and is tooling its silicon foundry to deliver chips singularly to execute that standard.13

There still are issues with interoperability among gadgets of distinctive makes that actualize the same specialized standard, however these are being determined gradually as an aftereffect of business sector weights. Be that as it may, it is vital to note that except for in reverse similarity from 802.11b to 802.11, gadgets utilizing the measures above are not interoperable (802.11a and 802.11h interoperability is yet to be determined).

Remote LAN Vulnerabilities and Risks

Notwithstanding all the vulnerabilities basic to wired systems, remote LANs present another arrangement of dangers. The basic vulnerabilities are listening stealthily, unlawful section into the system and dissent of administration. A few clients may see they are at danger from being presented to radio wave vitality, yet there is no valid examination supporting this theory, and US FCC Part 15 certificate obliges that gadgets meet the administration standard for presentation.

Since it is by a long shot the most mainstream remote LAN standard as of now, the accompanying examination will be restricted to the variations of the IEEE 802.11 standard. Just the specifics of vulnerabilities and execution examined thus are correlated to that arrangement of systems. The modalities of danger are the same for a wide range of remote LANs. As it were, every remote Lan face the same populace of dangers to message classifiedness, uprightness and validness as is confronted by the 802.11 arrangement. Just the specialized subtle elements of managing those dangers vary from standard to standard.

Spying

By their tendency, remote LANs emanate system activity into space. When that is done, it is difficult to control who can get the signs. Along these lines, it must be accepted in any remote LAN establishment that the system movement is liable to block attempt and spying by outsiders. The conspicuous answer for this issue is to scramble the information stream. The 802.11 measures accommodate doing decisively that. Tragically, the usage of this arrangement is not as much as great.

To give security on remote LANs, the 802.11b standard accommodates wired identical protection (WEP). WEP utilizes 40-bit static keys and RC4 encryption.14 There are a few issues with the usage of this methodology. In the first place, WEP is a choice. It is not enacted naturally in dispatched items, and it diminishes crude throughput by as much as 50 percent. To aggravate matters, it is generally accepted that numerous system heads are unconscious the element even exists. Thus, most working systems have not empowered WEP.15 In such a circumstance, the system is telecasting all system activity liberated for the advantage of all who can capture it. That is not really a protected method of operation. More regrettable, things being what they are WEP itself is lethally defective. A board of trustees of the IEEE in charge of WEP and different remote LAN guidelines has affirmed a fix for this imperfection.

The WEP way to deal with cryptography sounds secure: WEP encodes each bundle with an alternate key. Nonetheless, WEP does not appropriately execute the RC4 introduction vector. It utilizes a clear and unsurprising method for increasing the vector starting with one bundle then onto the next. Combined with powerless key administration and a confined key space, WEP is obviously unreliable. Ahead of schedule in 2001, specialists at the University of California, Berkeley (USA), if hypothetical verification that the WEP security plan could be broken.16 More late endeavors by different scientists utilizing those strategies succeeded as a part of breaking the key on a real system in a couple of hours the first occasion when they attempted, and in considerably less time on ensuing attempts.17 Researchers additionally have demonstrated to it is conceivable to listen to parcels, infuse bundles and modify bundles on remote LANs utilizing WEP.18 As if these discoveries were insufficient, the WEP watchword conspire likewise has been discovered to be imperfect with the outcome that a gatecrasher can get entrance to some WEP-secured systems in as meager as 30 seconds.19

The main driver of this issue has been accounted for as being singularly the RC4 encryption plan. Notwithstanding, a more precise portrayal is that WEP was made without careful understanding and open survey of the cryptographic primitives that were consolidated to shape it, and it is obliged to perform a few security capacities at the same time: validation, uprightness and confidentiality.20 The outcome is that WEP alone- - as it is exists at this composition - can't be depended upon to secure the remote system.

The IEEE has additionally proposed an overhauled standard, WEP2, to address these weaknesses. WEP2 utilizes 128-bit encryption and a 128-bit instatement vector. In any case, it still depends on RC4 encryption and still is surveyed as being helpless against the assaults portrayed previously.21 The IEEE has further embraced to characterize an improved security system standard that will utilize the recently received Advanced Encryption Standard (AES), which is supplanting the Digital Encryption Standard (DES) being used subsequent to the 1970s. Business items consolidating this new standard will be presented in 2002. Then again, similarity issues will remain.

There obviously are advances that can be utilized to give cryptographic level classifiedness past what is offered by WEP. The scientists who "broke" WEP suggest regarding every remote system as being outside the firewall and utilizing larger amount conventions, for example, SSH or IPSec, to give security. Another methodology is an overlaid exclusive cryptographic mapping in view of the MD5 calculation from NextComm.22 There surely will be different methodologies sooner rather than later. The issue is that these further diminish throughput, build many-sided quality, possibly include restrictive equipment and/or programming and lessen system usability for the end clients.

Amidst this troubling news about remote security, one ought to understand that total security was never the objective of WEP. Obviously, outright security is outlandish. The objective of WEP was to give a level of security comparable with that found on wired LANs. One can contend that, in spite of its cryptographic issues, WEP has accomplished that objective. Wired systems are not for the most part exceptionally secure unless secured by measures past those gave by the system conventions.

Numerous have encountered interfacing a PC to a wired LAN and being capable all of a sudden to get to assets to which they had no right.23 This is a typical issue, normally controlled by constraining which PCs might physically join with the LAN. Then again, in the remote space, it is more hard to restrict who can interface with the LAN, so WEP- - notwithstanding its weaknesses - is an imperative device in the general administration of system security.

Illegal Entry

Remote LANs could be utilized just to network altered PCs, subsequently staying away from the expenses of cabling. Ordinarily, on the other hand, they are utilized to interconnect very portable client populaces provisioned with PCs. The very way of the remote conventions is to make the system easy to use by encouraging association with an entrance point- - and in this way the whole system - as the client moves about. That is to say, the framework has powerless verification. One can think about the cell phone arrange as a harsh simple: the cell system would not be almost as valuable, if clients couldn't move about unreservedly in their home zones and far from home. Tragically, the very element that makes remote LANs so valuable additionally opens a noteworthy security gap.

Remote system hardware, as designed out of the case, is by and large situated so the system name is a default name for community and all system interface cards that adjust to the standard of the system (e.g., 802.11b) can promptly unite with the framework. Few system overseers try to change the level of access to something more prohibitive than the default. The remote access point publicizes its vicinity and its system name, and when a remote customer detects the entrance point, the customer endeavors to interface with the system. Unless the capacity to associate is by one means or another limited, the association endeavor will succeed, and another client will have been added to those effectively bolstered. As remote LANs basically serve to augment wired systems, the perspective this newcomer has of the system may be very broad, and the assets accessible may incorporate numerous not expected for easygoing guests. This is for all intents and purposes indistinguishable to the circumstance with wired systems. The distinction is that one must increase physical access to a wired system to interface with it. With a remote LAN, one just must be in the region. As it happens, the region may be fairly substantial.

Contingent upon the basic components in the way, a remote LAN sign may be usable for separations of give or take 500 meters. While this is useful from a scope viewpoint, it is not useful from a security outlook. Utilizing directional reception apparatuses, one can recognize remote system signals at separations up to eight miles (12.8 kilometers) from the system node.24 In such a circumstance, somebody can unite with a system from outside the border of a position of business and most likely without the association's information. The capacity of unapproved clients to join remote systems without identification has been exhibited over and again and has showed up in the standard media. One specialist has expressed openly that "hackers can venture to every part of the whole length of Market Street in San Francisco 'and essentially not lose 802.11 scope' while getting remote LAN motions in their cars."25 Software, unreservedly accessible on the Internet, promptly turns a tablet phone a remote system card into an instrument that recognizes remote systems, gives the client the system recognizable proof and data about encryption being utilized, and after that permits the client to sign into unprotected remote systems.

Vast systems that coddle vagrant clients are pretty much compelled to acknowledge the poor verification gave by WEP. It would not do if one needed to enlist ahead of time to utilize a system in an open air terminal space, for occurrence.

Notwithstanding, littler systems have an alternative that can offer assistance. It is conceivable to confine access to the system to those system hubs whose media access control (MAC) locations are known ahead of time by the entrance point. For little remote systems with a steady client populace, this is an alluring choice.

Denial of Service

A denial-of-service (DoS) attack is one wherein the attacker attempts to render the target network unable to serve its legitimate users. In the wired domain, many have become accustomed to protocol-based attacks, such as the "Ping of Death," which seek to overwhelm the target network with traffic forcing the network servers to crash. This type of attack also is effective against wireless networks.

In addition to protocol-based DoS attacks, wireless networks are vulnerable to a denial-of-service attack that is not viable against their wired brethren. Because their signals must travel through the public airwaves rather than in protected cables, wireless networks are extremely vulnerable to radio interference, either deliberate or accidental. Accidental interference occurs all too often owing to the shared nature of the bands in which these networks operate. It is very common for a wireless network, or a portion of it, to become unusable when a cordless telephone is operating in the same band and in physical proximity to the wireless node. It also is common for one wireless network to interfere with another nearby network, often making both useless.

Deliberate jamming attacks are not as common as accidental interference, but they are certainly straightforward. All that is required is to set up a transmitter covering the band where the wireless LAN operates and ensure that the transmitter has sufficient power to overwhelm the relatively weak LAN nodes. As it happens, the most ubiquitous occupant of the 2.4 GHz ISM band is the microwave oven. Microwave ovens are supposed to operate at a single frequency in that band, but their frequency stability is poor. A devious user can make the frequency stability deliberately worse, so that the oven frequency covers many of the channels assigned for use by the wireless LAN. Wireless network nodes operate at power outputs of no more than a watt and usually less. With minor modification, the typical microwave oven, which operates at power output levels of around 600 watts, can become a practical jammer for wireless LANs. When designing a wireless LAN, involving a competent radio engineer to do a survey of existing signals in the frequency band of interest and assessing the likelihood of introducing jammers into the vicinity is usually money well spent. Periodic resurveys are a wise precaution. Wireless LAN users must be sensitive to the potential for both deliberate and accidental interference and have a plan for dealing with interruptions this may cause.

CHAPTER 12: HACKING MOBILE DEVICES

Cellular telephones and tablets have get to be vital to big business and government systems going from little associations to Fortune 500 organizations and vast offices. Regularly, cellular telephone arrangements become naturally, embraced by multitudes of end-clients for helpful email access, and additionally by administrators and officials who need access to touchy authoritative assets from their favored individual cell phones. In different cases, cellular telephones and tablets have get to be basic frameworks for a wide assortment of generation applications from big business asset arranging (ERP) to venture administration.

For every last bit of its accommodation, on the other hand, the universal utilization of cell phones in the work spot and past has brought new security dangers. As dependence on these gadgets has developed exponentially, associations have immediately perceived that cell telephones and tablets need more noteworthy security executions than a basic screen defender and astute secret word. Whether an Apple iPhone or iPad, a Windows Phone, or an Android or BlackBerry telephone or tablet, these gadgets have turn out to be immensely alluring and defenseless focuses for accursed attackers. The utilization of such gadgets represents a variety of new dangers to associations, including:

1. Dispersed touchy information stockpiling and access systems
2. Absence of steady fix administration and firmware redesigns
3. High likelihood of the gadget being hacked, lost or stolen

Versatile code and applications are additionally presenting new roads for malware and information spillage, uncovering discriminating undertaking mysteries, protected innovation, and actually identifiable data resources for attackers. To further confound matters, today there basically are insufficient individuals with the security abilities expected to oversee cell telephone and tablet arrangements.

CHAPTER 13: HACKING OPERATING SYSTEMS

Microsoft Windows (with so much forms as Windows XP; Windows Server 2012; Windows 7; and the freshest flavor that numerous have yet to warm up to, Windows 8) is the most generally utilized working framework (OS) on the planet. It's likewise the most broadly mishandled. Is this in light of the fact that Microsoft couldn't care less as much about security as different OS sellers? The short answer is "no." Sure, various security imperfections were ignored — particularly in the Windows NT days — yet Microsoft items are so pervasive all through today's net-lives up to expectations that Microsoft is the least demanding merchant to single out; in this way Microsoft items regularly wind up in the terrible fellows' line of sight. The one positive about hackers is that they're driving the necessity for better security!

A considerable lot of the security imperfections in the features aren't new. They're variations of vulnerabilities that have been around for quite a while in UNIX and Linux, for example, the remote method call (RPC) vulnerabilities that the Blaster worm misused. You've heard the expression, "The more things change, the more they stick with it." That applies here, as well. Most Windows assaults are anticipate capable if the patches are appropriately connected. Therefore, poor security administration is frequently the genuine reason Windows assaults are effective, yet Microsoft takes the accuse and must convey the weight.

Notwithstanding the secret word assaults I cover in Chapter 7, numerous different assaults are conceivable against a Windows-based framework. Huge amounts of data can be removed from Windows by just joining with the framework over a net-work and utilizing apparatuses to haul out the data. A number of these tests don't even oblige you to be confirmed to the remote framework. All somebody with malignant purpose needs to discover on your system is a defenseless Windows computer with a default setup that's not ensured by such measures as an individual firewall and the most recent security patches.

When you begin jabbing around on your system, you may be astonished at what number of your Windows-based PCs has security vulnerabilities. Moreover, you'll be significantly more amazed at exactly that it is so natural to endeavor vulnerabilities to increase complete remote control of Windows by utilizing an instrument, for example, Metasploit. After you unite with a Windows framework and have a substantial username and secret key (by knowing it or determining it by utilizing the watchword breaking systems in Chapter 7 or different strategies illustrated in this chapter), you can burrow more profound and adventure different parts of Windows.

This section demonstrates to you best practices to test for probably the most basic assaults against the Windows OS and blueprints countermeasures to verify your frameworks are secure.

Presenting Windows Vulnerabilities

Given Windows' convenience, its undertaking prepared Active Directory administration, and the element rich .NET advancement stage, numerous associations have moved to the Microsoft stage for their systems administration and registering needs. Numerous organizations — particularly the little to medium-sized ones — depend exclusively on the Windows OS for system use. Numerous huge associations run discriminating servers, for example, web servers and database servers, on the Windows stage too. In the event that security vulnerabilities aren't tended to and oversaw appropriately, they can bring a system or a whole association to its knees.

At the point when Windows and other Microsoft programming are assaulted — particularly by a far reaching Internet-based worm or infection — a huge number of organizations and a great many PCs are influenced. Some surely understood assaults against Windows can prompt the accompanying issues:

✓　　Leakage of delicate data, including records containing health awareness data and Visa numbers

✓　　Passwords being split and used to do different assaults

✓　　Systems taken totally disconnected from the net by refusal of administration (DoS) assaults

✓   Full remote control being acquired

✓   Entire databases being ruined or erased

At the point when unsecured Windows-based frameworks are assaulted, genuine things can happen to an enormous number of PCs around the globe.

Picking Tools

Actually several Windows hacking and testing devices are accessible. The key is to locate a situated of devices that can do what you need and that you're comfortable utilizing.

Numerous security devices — including a portion of the apparatuses in this part — work with just certain adaptations of Windows. The latest adaptation of every instrument in this part is perfect with Windows XP and Windows 7, yet your mileage may fluctuate.

The more security instruments and other force client applications you introduce in Windows — particularly programs that tie into the system drivers and TCP/IP stack — the more flimsy Windows gets to be. I'm discussing moderate performance, blue screens of death, and general shakiness issues. Sadly, regularly the main fix is to reinstall Windows and every one of your applications. In the wake of revamping my portable PC at regular intervals, I at long last wised up and purchased a duplicate of VMware Workstation and a committed PC that I can garbage up with test-ing devices without stressing over it influencing my capacity to accomplish my other work. (Ok, the recollections of those DOS and Windows 3.x days when things were much less complex!)

Free Microsoft apparatuses

You can utilize the accompanying free Microsoft apparatuses to test your frameworks for various security shortcomings:

✓   Built-in Windows programs for NetBIOS and TCP/UDP administration enumeration, for example, these three:

- nbtstat for social event NetBIOS name table data

- netstat for showing open ports on the neighborhood Windows framework

- net for running different system based summons, including perspective ing shares on remote Windows frameworks and including client accounts after you pick up a remote summon brief by means of Metasploit

✓   Microsoft Baseline Security Analyzer (MBSA) (www.microsoft.com/technet/security/devices/ mbsahome.mspx) to test for missing patches and essential Windows security settings

✓   Sysinternals (http://technet.microsoft.com/en-us/sys internals/default.aspx) to jab, goad, and screen Windows administrations, procedures, and assets both

In with no reservations one evaluation instruments

In with no reservations one instruments perform a wide mixture of security tests, including the accompanying:

✓   Port examining

✓   OS fingerprinting

✓   Basic watchword splitting

✓   Detailed weakness mappings of the different security shortcomings that the instruments find on your Windows frameworks

I utilize these instruments in my work with great results:

✓   GFI LanGuard (www.gfi.com/system security-powerlessness scanner)

✓   QualysGuard (www.qualys.com)

Qualys' cloud application administration supplier/programming as an administration (whatever term you need to utilize nowadays) is anything but difficult to utilize. Just sign into the between face, give it the IP locations to filter, and instruct it to go. The administration has extremely definite and exact powerlessness testing — it's my unsurpassed most loved for net-work/OS weakness testing. Another scanner I've heard great things about is Rapid7's Nexpose (www.rapid7.com/weakness scanner.jsp).

Errand particular apparatuses

The accompanying instruments perform maybe a couple particular assignments. These apparatuses give point by point security evaluations of your Windows frameworks and understanding that you may not generally get from holding nothing back one appraisal devices:

✓   Metasploit (www.metasploit.com) for misusing vulnerabilities that such apparatuses as QualysGuard and Nexpose find to get remote order prompts, include clients, and a great deal more

✓   NetScanTools Pro (www.netscantools.com) for TCP port examining, ping ranges, and offer identification

✓ ShareEnum (http://technet.microsoft.com/en-us/sys internals/bb897442.aspx) for offer count

✓ TCPView (http://technet.microsoft.com/en-us/sysinternals/bb897437.aspx) to see TCP and UDP session data

✓ Winfo (www.ntsecurity.nu/tool stash/winfo) for invalid session enumeration to assemble such design data as security arrangements, neighborhood client records, and shares

Windows XP SP2 and later forms, and also Windows Server 2003 SP1 and later forms, have another "undocumented component" that can (and will) seriously restrain your system filtering rates: Only ten half-open TCP connections can be set aside a few minutes. In the event that you think your framework may be influenced by this, look at the Event ID 4226 Patcher apparatus (www.lvllord.de) for a hack to keep running on the Windows TCP/IP stack that will permit you to change the TCP half-open associations setting to a more reasonable number. The default is to change it to 50, which appears to function admirably.

Be cautioned that Microsoft doesn't bolster this hack. Having said that, I haven't experienced any difficulty with this hack by any means. Crippling the Windows Firewall (or other outsider firewall) can help speed things up, as well. In the event that conceivable, test on a devoted framework or virtual machine, in light of the fact that doing as such minimizes any effect your test outcomes may have on the other work you do on your PC.

Gathering Information about Your Windows Vulnerabilities

When you survey Windows vulnerabilities, begin by filtering your PCs to see what the awful gentlemen can see.

The endeavors in this section were keep running against Windows from inside a firewall. Unless I call attention to something else, all the tests in this part can be keep running against all forms of the Windows OS. The assaults in this section are sufficiently critical to warrant testing for, paying little mind to your present setup. Your outcomes may fluctuate from mine contingent upon the particular adaptation of Windows, patch levels, and other framework solidifying you've done.

Framework examining

A couple of clear procedures can distinguish shortcomings in Windows frameworks.

Testing

Begin gathering data about your Windows frameworks by running a beginning port sweep:

1. Run fundamental sweeps to discover which ports are open on every Windows framework:

Examine for TCP ports with a port checking device, for example, NetScanTools Pro. The NetScanTools Pro results in Figure 11-1 demonstrate a few possibly helpless ports open on a Windows 7 framework, including those for DNS (UDP port 53); the ever-prominent — and effortlessly hacked — NetBIOS (port 139); and SQL Server (UDP 1434).

2. Perform OS count, (for example, filtering for shares and particular OS adaptations) by utilizing an in with no reservations one appraisal instrument, for example, LanGuard.

On the off chance that you have to rapidly distinguish the particular adaptation of Windows that's running, you can utilize Nmap (http://nmap.org/download.html) with the - O choice, as indicated in Figure 11-3.

Different OS fingerprinting devices are accessible, however I've discovered Nmap to be a standout amongst the most exact.

3. Focus potential security vulnerabilities.

This is subjective and may shift from framework to framework, yet what you need to search for are fascinating administrations and applications and proceed from there.

CHAPTER 14: HACKING COMMUNICATION SYSTEMS

Communication frameworks, for example, email and Voice over IP (VoIP) regularly make vulnerabilities that individuals ignore. Why? Indeed, from my experience, informing programming — both at the server and customer level — is vulnerable in light of the fact that system overseers frequently accept that firewalls and antivirus programming are all that's expected to keep inconvenience away, or they basically disregard securing these frameworks out and out.

In this part, I demonstrate to you generally accepted methods to test for regular email and VoIP issues. I additionally framework key countermeasures to help keep these hacks against your frameworks.

Presenting Messaging System Vulnerabilities

Essentially every single informing application are hacking focuses on your system. Given the expansion and business reliance on email, pretty much anything is reasonable amusement. Likewise with VoIP. It's absolute terrifying what individuals with sick purpose can do with it.

With informing frameworks, one basic shortcomings is that a significant number of the sup-porting conventions weren't composed considering security — particularly those added to quite a few years prior when security wasn't almost the issue it is today. The interesting thing is that even advanced informing conventions — or at minimum the execution of the conventions — are still vulnerable to genuine security issues. Moreover, comfort and convenience regularly exceed the requirement for security.

Numerous assaults against informing frameworks are simply minor aggravations; others can deliver genuine mischief on your data and your association's notoriety. Malevolent assaults against informing frameworks incorporate the accompanying:

✓ Transmitting malware

✓ Crashing servers

✓ Obtaining remote control of workstations

✓ Capturing data while it traversed the system

✓ Perusing messages put away on servers and workstations

✓ Gathering informing pattern data through log records or a system analyzer that can tip off the attacker about discussions in the middle of individuals and associations (frequently called activity investigation or informal community examination)

✓ Capturing and replaying telephone discussions

✓   Gathering interior system setup data, for example, hostnames and IP addresses

These assaults can prompt such issues as unapproved — and conceivably illicit — divulgence of delicate data, and additionally loss of data through and through.

Perceiving and Countering E-Mail Attacks

The accompanying assaults misuse the most widely recognized email security vulnerabilities I've seen. The uplifting news is that you can take out or minimize a large portion of them to the point where your data is not at danger. You'll need to be cautious running these assaults against your email framework — particularly amid top activity times — so continue with alert!

Some of these assaults require the fundamental hacking techniques: gathering open data, examining and listing your frameworks, and discovering and abusing the vulnerabilities. Others can be done by sending messages or catching system movement.

Email bombs

E-mail bombs assault by making dissent of administration (DoS) conditions against your email programming and even your system and Internet association by taking up a lot of data transmission and, infrequently, obliging a lot of storage room. Email bombs can crash a server and give unapproved head access.

Connections

An attacker can make a connection over-burden assault by sending hundreds or a great many messages with expansive connections to one or more recipients on your system.

Assaults utilizing email connections

Connection assaults have a few objectives:

✓ The entire email server may be focused for a complete interference of administration with these disappointments:

• Storage over-burden: Multiple vast messages can rapidly fill the aggregate stockpiling limit of an email server. On the off chance that the messages aren't automatically erased by the server or physically erased by individual client accounts, the server will be not able to get new messages.

This can make a genuine DoS issue for your email framework, either smashing it or obliging you to take your framework disconnected from the net to tidy up the garbage that has collected. A 100MB document connection sent ten times to 100 clients can take 100GB of storage room. Wow!

• Bandwidth obstructing: An attacker can crash your email administration or convey it to a slither by filling the approaching Internet association with garbage. Regardless of the possibility that your framework naturally distinguishes and tosses evident connection assaults, the false messages eat assets and deferral preparing of legitimate messages.

✓   An assault on a solitary email location can have genuine results if the location is for an essential client or gathering.

Countermeasures against email connection assaults

These countermeasures can help avert connection over-burden assaults:

✓   Limit the measure of either messages or email connections. Weigh for this alternative in your email server's arrangement settings, (for example, those master vided in Novell GroupWise and Microsoft Exchange), your email substance sifting framework, and even at the email customer level.

✓ Limit every client's space on the server. This denies extensive connections from being composed to plate. Farthest point message sizes for inbound and even outbound messages if you need to keep a client from dispatching this assault from inside your system. I locate a couple of gigabytes is a decent cutoff, however it all relies on upon your system size, stockpiling accessibility, business culture, et cetera, so thoroughly consider this one deliberately before put-ting anything set up.

Consider utilizing SFTP or HTTP rather than email for substantial document exchanges. There are various cloud-based record exchange administrations accessible. You can likewise urge your clients to utilize departmental shares or open organizers. Thusly, you can store one duplicate of the document on a server and have the beneficiary download the record on his or her own workstation.

In opposition to mainstream thinking and utilize, the email framework ought not be an information storehouse, but rather that's precisely what email has advanced into. An email server utilized for this reason can make superfluous lawful and administrative dangers and can transform into an outright bad dream if your business gets an e-revelation solicitation identified with a claim. A vital piece of your data security program is to add to a data characterization and maintenance project to help with records administration. Be that as it may, don't go only it. Get others, for example, your legal counselor, HR administrator, and CIO included. This helps spread the responsibility around and guarantees your business doesn't cause harm for holding too much — or excessively few — electronic records in the case of a claim or examination.

Associations

A hacker can send a colossal number of messages at the same time to addresses on your system. These association assaults can bring about the server to abandon adjusting any inbound or outbound TCP asks. This circumstance can prompt a complete server lockup or an accident, frequently bringing about a condition in which the attacker is permitted overseer or root access to the framework.

Assaults utilizing surges of messages

An assault utilizing a surge of messages is regularly completed in spam assaults and other foreswearing of administration endeavors.

Countermeasures against association assaults

Forestall email assaults as far out on your system border as you can. The more activity or malevolent conduct you keep off your email servers and clients, the better.

Numerous email servers permit you to restrain the quantity of assets utilized for inbound associations, as indicated in the Number of SMTP Receive Threads alternative for Novell GroupWise. This setting is called distinctive things for diverse email servers and email firewalls, so check your documentation.

Totally halting a boundless number of inbound solicitations is incomprehensible. Nonetheless, you can minimize the effect of the assault. This setting confines the measure of server

CHAPTER 15: HACKING WEBSITES

Websites and web applications are normal focuses for assault in light of the fact that they're all around and frequently open for anybody to jab and nudge.

Essential sites utilized for showcasing, contact data, report down-burdens, thus on are particularly simple for the awful gentlemen to play around with. In any case, for criminal hackers, sites that give a front end to complex applications and databases that store important data, for example, charge card and Social Security numbers, are particularly appealing. This is the place the cash is, both actually and allegorically.

Why are sites and applications so powerless? The agreement is that they're defenseless in view of poor programming improvement and testing practices. Sound recognizable? It ought to; this same issue influences working frameworks and basically all parts of PC frameworks. This is the reaction of depending on programming compilers to perform lapse checking, melting away client interest for higher-quality programming, and stressing time-to-market rather than security and quality.

This part exhibits site and application tests to keep running on your frameworks. Given all the custom programming design conceivable outcomes, you can test for actually a huge number of web vulnerabilities. In this section, I concentrate on the ones I see regularly utilizing both robotized scanners and manual investigation. I likewise layout countermeasures to help minimize the chances that somebody with sick expectation can complete these assaults against what are likely viewed as your most basic frameworks.

I need to call attention to that this section just skims the surface of all conceivable web security defects and approaches to test for them. Extra hotspots for building your web security testing aptitudes are the apparatuses and benchmarks, (for example, the Top 10 Web Application Security Risks) gave by the Open Web Application Security Project (www.owasp.org).

Picking Your Web Application Tools

Great web weakness scanners and related apparatuses can help guarantee that you take full advantage of your sweeps. Likewise with numerous things in life, I observe that you get what you pay for regarding testing for web security openings. This is the reason I basically utilize business instruments in my work when testing sites and web applications for vulnerabilities.

These are my most loved web security testing apparatuses:

✓   Acunetix Web Vulnerability Scanner (www.acunetix.com) for in with no reservations one security testing, including a port scanner, a HTTP sniffer, and a computerized SQL infusion apparatus

✓ Firefox Web Developer (http://chrispederick.com/work/web-designer) for manual investigation and control of pages

Yes, you must do manual examination. You without a doubt need to utilize a scanner, on the grounds that scanners find around a large portion of the issues. For the other half, you have to do significantly more than simply run computerized filtering devices. Keep in mind that you need to get where scanners leave off to genuinely survey the general security of your sites and applications. You need to do some manual work not on the grounds that web weakness scanners are broken, but rather in light of the fact that jabbing and pushing web frameworks basically oblige great out-dated hacker dishonesty and your most loved web program.

✓　　HTTrack Website Copier (www.httrack.com) for reflecting a webpage for logged off assessment

Reflecting is a system for creeping through (additionally called spidering) a site's each niche and crevice and downloading freely open pages to your nearby framework.

✓　　WebInspect (www.hpenterprisesecurity.com/items/hp-sustain programming security-focus/hp-webinspect) for in with no reservations one security testing, including an astounding HTTP intermediary and HTTP proofreader and a robotized SQL infusion apparatus

You can likewise utilize general weakness scanners, for example, QualysGuard and

LanGuard, and endeavor devices, for example, Metasploit, when testing web servers and applications. You can utilize these instruments to discover (and misuse) frail nesses that you may not generally find with standard web-filtering apparatuses and manual investigation. Google can be useful for establishing through web applications and searching for delicate data also. Despite the fact that these non– application-particular instruments can be advantageous, it's essential to realize that they won't penetrate down as profound as the apparatuses I say in the first rundown.

Contextual analysis in hacking web applications with Caleb Sima

For this situation study, Caleb Sima, a surely understood application security master, shared an ordeal of performing a web-application security test.

The Situation

Mr. Sima was employed to perform a web application penetration test to evaluate the security of a no doubt understood monetary site. Furnished with simply the URL of the principle budgetary site, Mr. Sima set out to discover what different destinations existed for the association and started by utilizing Google to hunt down potential outcomes. Mr. Sima at first ran a mechanized output against the principle servers to dis-cover any low-hanging natural product. This output gave data on the web server variant and some other essential data yet nothing that demonstrated valuable without further research. While Mr. Sima performed the output, neither the IDS nor the flame divider saw any of his movement. At that point Mr. Sima issued a solicitation to the server on the beginning page, which gave back some fascinating information. The web application had all the earmarks of being acknowledge ing numerous parameters, yet as Mr. Sima kept on skimming the site, he saw that the parameters in the URL finished what had been started. Mr. Sima chose to erase all the parameters inside of the URL to see what data the server would return when questioned. The server reacted with a mistake message depicting the kind of application environment.

Next, Mr. Sima performed a Google seek on the application that brought about some definite documentation. Mr. Sima discovered a few articles and tech notes inside of this data that demonstrated to him how the application functioned and what default records may exist. Actually, the server had a few of these default documents. Mr. Sima utilized this data to test the application further. He rapidly dis-secured interior IP locations and what administrations the application was putting forth. When Mr. Sima knew precisely what form the administrator was running, he needed to see what else he could discover.

Mr. Sima kept on controlling the URL from the application by including & characters inside of the announcement to control the custom script. This method permitted him to catch all source code documents. Mr. Sima noticed some between esting filenames, including VerifyLogin. htm ,ApplicationDetail. htm , CreditReport.htm , and ChangePassword.htm. At that point Mr. Sima attempted to interface with every document by issuing a specially organized URL to the server. The server gave back a User not signed in message for every solicitation and expressed that the association must be produced using the intranet.

The Outcome

Mr. Sima knew where the records were found and had the capacity sniff the association and prevent mine that the ApplicationDetail.htm record set a treat string. With little control of the URL, Mr. Sima hit the bonanza. This document returned customer data and Visas when another client application was being prepared. CreditReport.htm permitted Mr. Sima to view client credit report status, misrepresentation data, declined-application status, and a huge number of other touchy data. The lesson: Hackers can use numerous sorts of data to get through web applications. The individual adventures for this situation study were minor, however when joined, they brought about extreme vulnerabilities.

Caleb Sima was a contract individual from the X-Force group at Internet Security Systems and was the first individual from the penetration test-ing group. Mr. Sima went ahead to help establish SPI Dynamics (later procured by HP) and turn into its CTO, and in addition chief of SPI Labs, the application-security innovative work assemble inside SPI Dynamics.

Looking for Web Vulnerabilities

Assaults against unsecured sites and applications by means of Hypertext Transfer Protocol (HTTP) make up the lion's share of all Internet-related assaults. The greater part of these assaults can be completed regardless of the possibility that the HTTP activity is scrambled (through HTTPS or by means of HTTP over SSL) on the grounds that the interchanges medium has nothing to do with these assaults. The security vulnerabilities really exist in the sites and applications themselves or the web server and program programming that the frameworks keep running on and speak with.

Numerous assaults against sites and applications are simply minor irritations and may not influence delicate data or framework accessibility. In any case, a few assaults can wreak ruin on your frameworks, putting delicate data at danger and notwithstanding setting your association out of agreeability with state, government, and universal data security and security laws and regulations.

Catalog traversal

I begin you out with a straightforward registry traversal assault. Catalog traversal is a truly fundamental shortcoming, however it can turn up intriguing — now and again delicate — data around a web framework. This assault includes perusing a site and searching for signs about the server's index structure and delicate documents that may have been stacked deliberately or inadvertently.

Perform the accompanying tests to focus data about your site's registry structure.

Crawlers

A bug system, for example, the free HTTrack Website Copier, can creep your website to search for each freely available record. To utilize HTTrack, just load it, give your task a name, tell HTTrack which website(s) to reflect, and following a couple of minutes, perhaps hours (contingent upon the size and multifaceted nature of the webpage), you'll have everything that's openly available on the website put away on your neighborhood drive in c:\My Web Sites. Figure 14-1 demonstrates the slither yield of an essential site.

Muddled destinations frequently uncover more data that ought not be there, including old information records and even application scripts and source code.

Google

Google, the web index organization that numerous affection to hate, can likewise be utilized for catalog traversal. Indeed, Google's propelled inquiries are powerful to the point that you can utilize them to find touchy data, discriminating web server records and registries, Visa numbers, webcams — fundamentally anything that Google has found on your webpage — without needing to reflect your website and filter through everything physically. It's as of now staying there in Google's reserve holding up to be seen.

The accompanying are several best in class Google inquiries that you can enter straightforwardly into the Google pursuit field:

✓ site:hostname essential words — This question looks for any pivotal word you rundown, for example, SSN, secret, charge card, et cetera. An illustration would be:

✓ filetype:file-augmentationsite:hostname — This question looks for particular record sorts on a particular site, for example, doc, pdf, db, dbf, zip, and that's just the beginning. These record sorts may contain touchy data. A case would be:

Other progressed Google administrators incorporate the accompanying:

✓   allintitle hunt down magic words in the title of a page.

✓   inurl hunt down magic words in the URL of a page.

✓   related discovers pages like this page.

✓   link shows different locales that connection to this website page.

Particular definitions and more can be found at www.googleguide.com/advanced_operators.htm l. Likewise, a phenomenal asset for Google hacking is Johnny Long's Google Hacking Database (GHDB) site http://johnny. ihackstuff.com/ghdb. Extra hacking-related Google inquiries can be found at http://artkast.yak.net/81.

At the point when filtering through your site with Google, make certain to search for delicate data about your servers, system, and association in Google Groups (http://groups.google.com), which is the Usenet file. I have discovered representative postings in newsgroups that uncover a lot about the inner system and business frameworks — the sky is the breaking point. On the off chance that you discover something that doesn't should be there, you can work with Google to have it altered or evacuated. For more data, allude to Google's Contact us page at www. google.com/intl/en/contact.

Taking a gander at the broad view of web security, Google hacking is really restricted, yet in the event that you're truly into it, look at Johnny Long's book, Google Hacking for Penetration Testers (Syngress).

Countermeasures against index traversals

You can utilize three primary countermeasures against having documents compromised through vindictive catalog traversals:

✓ Don't store old, touchy, or generally nonpublic documents on your web server. The main documents that ought to be in your/htdocs or DocumentRoot envelope are those that are required for the site to work legitimately. These documents ought not contain classified data that you don't need the world to see.

✓ Configure your robots.txt record to forestall internet searchers, for example, Google, from creeping the more touchy regions of your website.

✓ Ensure that your web server is legitimately designed to permit free to just those indexes that are required for the webpage to function. Least benefits are key here, so give access to just the documents and indexes required for the web application to perform legitimately.

Check your web server's documentation for guidelines on controlling free. Contingent upon your web server form, these entrance controls are situated in

- The httpd.conf document and the .htaccess records for Apache (See http://httpd.apache.org/docs/configuring.html for more data.)

- Internet Information Services Manager for IIS

The most recent adaptations of these web servers have great catalog security of course thus, if conceivable, verify you're running the most recent renditions.

At last, think about utilizing as an internet searcher honeypot, for example, the Google Hack Honeypot (http://ghh.sourceforge.net). A honey pot attracts malicious clients so you can perceive how the awful fellows are conflicting with your site. At that point, you can utilize the learning you pick up to keep them under control.

CHAPTER 16: HACKING APPLICATIONS

Data sifting assaults

Sites and applications are infamous for taking for all intents and purposes any sort of info, erroneously accepting that its legitimate, and preparing it promote. Not validating info is one of the best slip-ups that web engineers can make.

A few assaults that embed deformed information — regularly, a lot at one time — can be keep running against a site or application, which can confound the framework and make it reveal an excessive amount of data to the attacker. Information assaults can likewise make it simple for the terrible gentlemen to gather delicate data from the web programs of clueless clients.

Cradle floods

A standout amongst the most genuine info assaults is a support flood that particularly targets data handle in web applications.

For example, a credit-reporting application may validate clients before they're permitted to submit information or draw reports. The login structure utilizes the take after ing code to get client IDs with a most extreme information of 12 characters, as meant by the maxsize variable:

A commonplace login session would include a substantial login name of 12 characters or less. In any case, the maxsize variable can be changed to something immense, for example, 100 or even 1,000. At that point an attacker can enter sham information in the login field. What happens next is anybody's call — the application may hang, over-compose other information in memory, or accident the server.

A basic approach to control such a variable is to venture through the page accommodation by utilizing a web intermediary, for example, those implicit to the commercial web powerlessness scanners I specify or the free Paros Proxy (www. parosproxy.org).

Web intermediaries sit between your web program and the server you're testing and permit you to control data sent to the server. To start, you must arrange your web program to utilize the neighborhood intermediary of 127.0.0.1 on port 8080.

In Firefox, this is open by picking Tools⇨Options; snap Advanced, click the Network tab, tap the Connection Settings catch, and afterward select the Manual Proxy Configuration radio catch. In Internet Explorer, pick

Tools⇨Internet Options; tap the Connections tab, tap the LAN Settings

Catch, and afterward select the Use a Proxy Server for Your LAN check box.

You should simply change the field length of the variable before your program presents the page, and it will be submitted utilizing whatever length you give. You can likewise utilize the Firefox Web Developer to uproot most extreme structure lengths characterized in web shapes.

Utilizing Firefox Web Developer to reset structure field lengths

URL control

A computerized data assault controls a URL and sends it back to the server, advising the web application to do different things, for example, sidetrack to outsider destinations, load touchy documents off the server, et cetera. Neighborhood document inclusion is one such defenselessness. This is the point at which the web application acknowledges URL-based info and returns the predetermined record's substance to the client. For instance, in one circumstance, WebInspect sent something like the accompanying demand and gave back the Linux server's passwd record:

The accompanying connections exhibit another illustration of URL slyness called URL redirection:

In both circumstances, an attacker can abuse this defenselessness by sending the connection to clueless clients through email or by posting it on a site. At the point when clients tap the connection, they can be diverted to a malignant outsider site containing malware or wrong material.

In the event that you don't have anything yet time staring you in the face, you may reveal these sorts of vulnerabilities physically. Nonetheless, in light of a legitimate concern for rational soundness (and exactness), these assaults are best completed by running a web defenselessness scanner on the grounds that they can identify the shortcoming by sending hundreds and several URL emphases to the web framework rapidly.

Concealed field control

A few sites and applications insert concealed fields inside of pages to pass state data between the web server and the program. Shrouded fields are spoken to in a web shape as <input type="hidden">. Due to poor coding practices, shrouded fields regularly contain private data, (for example, item costs on an e-trade site) that ought to be put away just in a back-end database. Clients shouldn't see shrouded fields — consequently the name — yet the inquisitive attacker can find and adventure them with these strides:

1.   View the HTML source code.

To see the source code in Internet Explorer, pick Page⇨View Source. In Firefox, pick View⇨Page Source.

2.   Change the data put away in these fields.

Case in point, a malevolent client may change the cost from $100 to $10.

3.   Repost the page back to the server.

This stride permits the attacker to acquire sick gotten increases, for example, a lower cost on a web buy.

Utilizing concealed fields for validation (login) components can be particularly hazardous. I once went over a multifaceted confirmation interloper lockout prepare that depended on a shrouded field to track the quantity of times the client endeavored to sign in. This variable could be reset to zero for each login endeavor and hence encourage a scripted lexicon or beast power login assault. It was somewhat unexpected that the security control to forestall gatecrasher assaults was vulnerable to an interloper assault.

A few instruments, for example, Web Proxy (which accompanies WebInspect) or Paros Proxy, can undoubtedly control shrouded fields. Figure 14-3 shows SPI Proxy's interface and a website page's shrouded field.

CHAPTER 17: HACKING DATABASES

Attacks against databases and capacity frameworks can be intense in light of the fact that that's the place "the merchandise" are found, and the terrible fellows are very much aware of that. These assaults can happen over the Internet or on the inner system when outer attackers and noxious insiders misuse any number of vulnerabilities. These assaults can likewise happen through the web application through SQL infusion.

Plunging into Databases

Database frameworks, for example, Microsoft SQL Server, MySQL, and Oracle, have hidden off camera, however their worth and their vulnerabilities have at last go to the bleeding edge. Yes, even the strong Oracle that was once guaranteed to be unhackable is powerless to comparable adventures as its rival. With the huge number of administrative necessities administering database security, scarcely any business can avoid the dangers that exist in on the grounds that for all intents and purposes each business (extensive and little) utilizes a database.

Picking instruments

Likewise with remote, working frameworks, etc, you require great apparatuses in case you're going to discover the database security issues that number. The accompanying are my most loved instruments for testing database security:

✓   Advanced SQL Password Recovery (www.elcomsoft.com/asqlpr. html) for splitting Microsoft SQL Server passwords

✓   Cain & Abel (www.oxid.it/cain.html) for splitting database password hashes

✓ QualysGuard (www.qualys.com) for performing inside and out powerlessness filters

✓ SQLPing3 (www.sqlsecurity.com/downloads) for finding Microsoft SQL Servers on the system, checking for clear sa (the default SQL Server framework head account) passwords, and performing word reference watchword breaking assaults

You can likewise utilize adventure devices, for example, Metasploit, for your database testing.

Discovering databases on the system

The initial phase in finding database vulnerabilities is to make sense of where they're situated on your system. It sounds amusing, yet numerous system administrators I've met aren't even mindful of different databases running in their environments. This is particularly valid for the free SQL Server Express database delicate product that anybody can download and keep running on a workstation or test framework.

I can't let you know how frequently I discover touchy generation information, for example, charge card and Social Security numbers, being utilized as a part of test databases that are totally completely open to mishandle by inquisitive insiders. Utilizing delicate information as a part of the uncontrolled regions of improvement and quality affirmation (QA) is an information rupture hold up ing to happen.

The best device I've found to find Microsoft SQL Server frameworks is SQLPing3

A contextual analysis in hacking databases with Chip Andrews

The Situation

Amid a normal penetration test, Mr. Andrews performed the compulsory Google looks, area name exploration, working framework balance gerprinting, and port sweeps, however this specific site was secured tight. Proceeding onward to the electronic application running on the framework, he was promptly stood up to with a login page utilizing SSL-scrambled structures authentication. By checking the wellspring of the website page, he saw that a concealed App_Name field was being gone to the application at whatever point a client endeavored to sign into the webpage. Might it be able to be that the designers may have neglected to perform legitimate data acceptance on this pure looking parameter? The chase was on.

The Outcome

First and foremost, the time had come to amass the tool stash. At the season of this penetration test, Mr. Andrews wanted to utilize the accompanying: Paros Proxy, Absinthe, Cain & Abel, Data Thief, and the Microsoft SQL Server Management Studio/SQL Server (Express Edition), all of which are benefit capable free.

First off, he utilized Paros Proxy to take into consideration more control and perceivability to the web solicitations made to the web server. After arachnid ing the site for accessible pages and performing a snappy weakness check for SQL infusion, it was affirmed that the App_Name parameter seemed to bring about the application to toss an Error 500 special case, showing an application disappointment. Penetration tests are one of the uncommon events when an application disappointment is an alluring result.

Since the application disappointment demonstrated that Mr. Andrews could infuse unintended burn acters into the SQL code being sent from the application to the database, he could see whether it was an exploitable condition. A typical test that works with Microsoft SQL Server databases is to infuse a charge, for example, WAITFOR DELAY '00:00:10', which causes the database server to slow down for 10 seconds. In an application that ordinarily gives back a page in one second or less, a steady 10-second defer is a decent pointer that you can infuse charges into the SQL stream.

Next, Mr. Andrews endeavored to utilize the Data Thief device to assault the login page. This apparatus endeavors to constrain the database to utilize an OPENROWSET order to duplicate information from the objective database to Mr. Andrews' database situated on the Internet. This is generally an exceptionally effective approach to siphon a lot of information from powerless databases, however for this situation, his assault was thwarted! The database manager at the objective had incapacitated the OPENROWSET usefulness by legitimately designing the Disable Adhoc Distributed Queries alternative.

With industriousness as his watchword, Mr. Andrews persevered with the following apparatus — Absinthe. This apparatus utilizes a procedure called visually impaired SQL injection to make determinations about information utilizing straightforward yes or no inquiries of the database. For instance, the device may ask the database whether the first letter of a table is not as much as "L." If yes, the application may do nothing, yet in the event that no, the application may toss a special case. Utilizing this basic paired rationale, it is conceivable to utilize this strategy to uncover the whole database structure and even the information put away inside — yet gradually. Utilizing the device, he recognized a table of delicate client data and downloaded a few hundred records to demonstrate the customer.

(proceeded)

SQLPing3 can find occasions of SQL Server holed up behind individual flame dividers and that's only the tip of the iceberg — an element previously just accessible in SQLPing2's sister appli-cationSQLRecon.

In the event that you have Oracle in your surroundings, Pete Finnigan has an incredible rundown of Oracle-driven security instruments at www.petefinnigan.com/tools.htm that can perform capacities like SQLPing3.

Breaking database passwords

SQLPing3 additionally serves as a pleasant word reference based SQL Server watchword breaking system. As should be obvious in Figure 15-1, it checks for clear sa passwords naturally. Another free apparatus for breaking SQL Server, MySQL, and Oracle secret word hashes is Cain & Abel.

The business item Elcomsoft Distributed Password Recovery (www. elcomsoft.com/edpr.html) can likewise break Oracle watchword hashes.

In the event that you have admittance to SQL Server master.mdf documents, you can utilize Elcomsoft's Advanced SQL Password Recovery (www.elcomsoft.com/asqlpr.html) to recuperate database passwords quickly.

You may discover some legacy Microsoft Access database documents that are secret word secured too. No stresses: The instrument Advanced Office

Secret word Recovery (www.elcomsoft.com/acpr.html) can get you right in.

As you can envision, these secret word breaking apparatuses are an incredible approach to demonstrate the most fundamental of shortcomings in your database security. One of the most ideal approaches to go about demonstrating that there's an issue is to utilize Microsoft SQL Server 2008 Management Studio Express (www.microsoft.com/en-us/download/details.aspx?id=7593) to associate with the database frameworks you now have the passwords for and set up secondary passage records or peruse around to see what's accessible. In essentially every unprotected SQL Server framework I go over, there's delicate individual money related or human services information accessible for the taking.

Examining databases for vulnerabilities

Likewise with working frameworks and web applications, some database-particular vulnerabilities can be found just by utilizing the right apparatuses. I utilize QualysGuard to discover such issues as

✓ Buffer floods

✓ Privilege accelerations

✓ Password hashes open through default/unprotected records

✓ Weak confirmation systems empowered

✓ Database audience log documents that can be renamed without confirmation

An extraordinary holding nothing back one business database powerlessness scanner for performing inside and out database checks — including client rights reviews on SQL Server, Oracle, etc — is AppDetectivePro (www.appsecinc.com/items/appdetective/). AppDetectivePro can be a decent expansion to your security testing instrument stockpile in the event that you can legitimize the speculation.

Numerous vulnerabilities can be tried from both an unauthenticated untouchable's viewpoint and also a believed insider's point of view. For instance, you can utilize the SYSTEM represent Oracle to sign in, specify, and output the framework (something that QualysGuard bolsters). My fingers are crossed that Qualys will inevitably bolster confirmed sweeps for SQL Server.

Taking after Best Practices for Minimizing Database Security Risks

Keeping your databases secure is really straightforward on the off chance that you do the accompanying:

✓ Run your databases on distinctive machines.

✓ Check the fundamental working frameworks for security vulnerabilities. I cover working framework abuses for Windows and Linux in Chapters 11 and 12, individually.

✓ Ensure that your databases fall inside of the extent of fixing and framework solidifying.

✓ Require solid passwords on every database framework.

✓ Use proper record and offer

CHAPTER 18: HACKING FREE SOFTWARE DOWNLOADS, FREE WIFI AND HOTMAIL

Free hacking software

Instructions to Become a Free Software Hacker

Composing and utilizing Free software is not only a kind of programming, it is a sort of rationality. While knowing a programming dialect is everything you need to program, this article is about how to join the group, get companions, do awesome cooperate, and turn into a regarded authority with a profile you can't go anyplace else. In the realm of Free software you might rather effectively get errands that in an organization just the world class, top level developers are permitted to do. Consider the measure of experience this can bring. In any case, in the event that you once chose to turn into a Free software programmer, you must be prepared to put sooner or later into accomplishing this objective. This remaining parts genuine regardless of the possibility that you are an IT understudy as of now. Likewise, this article is not about how to turn into a saltine.

Steps

1. Get a decent Unix dissemination. GNU/Linux is a standout amongst the most mainstream for hacking yet GNU Hurd, BSD, Solaris and (to some degree) Mac OS X are frequently utilized.

2. Figure out how to utilize Command Line. You can do a great deal more with Unix like working frameworks in the event that you utilize charge line.

3. Realize some prominent programming dialect until you achieve a pretty much palatable level. Without this, you can't contribute code (the most essential piece of any software undertaking) to the free software group. A few sources recommend to start without a moment's delay with two dialects: one framework dialect (C, Java or comparative) and one scripting

dialect (Python, Ruby, Perl or comparable).

4. To be more gainful, learn Eclipse or some other comparative incorporated improvement device.

5. Learn and utilization propelled supervisor like VI or Emacs. They have higher expectation to learn and adapt yet you can do substantially more with them.

6. Learn from control. Adaptation control is likely the most critical co-operation apparatus for shared software advancement. See how to make and apply fixes (content contrast documents). Most Free software advancement in the group is done making, talking about and applying different patches.

7. Locate a suitable little Free software venture which you could without much of a stretch join to get experience. The greater part of such undertakings now can be found on SourceForge.net. The suitable task must:

- Utilize the programming dialect you know.
- Be dynamic, with late discharges.
- As of now have three to five designers.
- Use form control.

Have some part you think you can promptly begin actualizing without altering the current code excessively.

Aside from the code, a great venture likewise has dynamic examination records, bug reports, gets and actualizes demands for improvement and shows other comparable exercises.

8. Contact the overseer of the chose venture. In a little venture with couple of engineers your assistance will typically be promptly acknowledged.

9. Precisely read the principles of the task and pretty much tail them. The principles of the coding style or need to archive your adjustments in a different content

document might first seem ludicrous to you. However the reason for these guidelines is to make the common work conceivable - and the most tasks do have them.

10. Work in this task for a while. Listen deliberately that the chairman and other task individuals say. Separated programming, you have a considerable measure of things to learn. Be that as it may, in the event that you truly don't care for something, simply go away to another venture.

11. Try not to stay with the underground venture for a really long time. When you discover yourself effectively meeting expectations in that group, the time it now, time to search for the genuine one.

12. Locate a genuine, abnormal state Free software or Open source venture. Most such activities are possessed by GNU or Apache associations.

13. Right now doing a genuine bounce now, be prepared for the far cooler acknowledgment. You will probably be approached to work for quite a while without direct compose access to the code storehouse. The past underground venture ought to, nonetheless, have taught you a considerable measure - so following a while of the gainful commitment you can attempt to request rights you think you ought to have.

14. Take and do a genuine assignment. The time it now, time. Try not to be apprehensive. Go on even after you find that the assignment is parcels more troublesome than you at first thought - in this stride it is essential not to surrender.

15. In the event that you can, apply with your genuine errand to the Google's "Mid year of Code" to get some cash from this experience. However, simply couldn't care less if the application is not acknowledged

as they have far less supported positions than okay programmers.

16. Search for a suitable meeting occurrence adjacent ("Linux days" or something comparable) and attempt to show your task there (all undertaking, not simply the part you are modifying). After you let you know are speaking to a genuine Free/Open source extend, the coordinators oftentimes discharge you from the gathering expense (in the event that they don't, the meeting is likely inadmissible at any rate). Bring your Linux portable PC (in the event that you have one) and run demos. Approach the task director for the material you may utilize when setting up your discussion or blurb.

17. Hunt the web down declaration about the introduce gathering occurrence adjacent and attempt to go along with it first time presently (look for all issues and how

programmers tackle them) and next time at this very moment.

18. Complete the assignment, spread with programmed tests and add to the undertaking. You are finished! Undoubtedly, attempt to meet a few programmers of the undertaking physically and have a glass of lager.

19. For better comprehension, investigate genuine sample of the improvement history for a Free Software venture (above). Every raising bend speaks to a commitment (lines of code) from single designer. Designers have a tendency to end up less dynamic over years yet the undertaking habitually even quickens at this very moment join. Subsequently on the off chance that you as of now accompany some valuable aptitudes, there are no reasons why the group would not welcome you.

Free WiFi hacking

You have your PC secured with firewalls and against infection programs. That is incredible. How secured is the information you are conveying. Which would be the most agonizing, traumatic, and the most extravagant misfortune? The PC equipment itself, or the data programmers recover from the information?

This information can be accustomed to convey damage to you, your family, and your property. Each photo you or your kids send to their companions, and the world to see has GPS coordinates that pinpoint the area within three feet of where it was taken. Do you truly need undesirable interlopers to know which some piece of the play area your grandchildren support, or what school they go to, or where they go for entertainment, or where they live?

In the event that you:

- Utilize an advanced cell or computerized camera to take pictures
- Use WiFi, Google, Twitter or Facebook

- Transfer, send or email pictures in any structure over the web
- Your family could be the objectives of predators on the web.

Did You Know! There are anything but difficult to download programs that will permit very nearly ANYONE in under 5 minutes to:

- Take your private passwords.
- Take your Social Security Number.
- Take your charge card data.
- Take your saving money record numbers and passwords

Pinpoint to within three feet of where you took your transferred photographs

Also, EMPTY YOUR BANK ACCOUNT!

I did a Google look for "free WiFi hacking software" and the outcomes were around 1,570,000 in 0.32 seconds. The danger is genuine.

Notwithstanding people or families numerous little organizations are not mindful of the dangers or they imagine that assurance is not accessible at a sensible cost.

Here is a powerlessness review to help you investigate your danger

Does your business at present utilize a VPN (Virtual Private Network) security system for remote access to your organization's system? Yes____ No____ No=20

Do you have representatives that telecommute or travel and utilize their cell phones or tablets to send/convey classified data information to the home office? Yes____ No____ Yes=10

Is it accurate to say that you are mindful that your representatives that get to your system servers through remote hotspots, for example, WiFi in inns, air terminals, and coffeehouses are most powerless against hack assaults which can prompt your secret data being stolen? Yes____ No____ No=10

Does your business store or send delicate information that would be profitable to digital offenders, for example, restrictive data about your organization, representatives, or clients? Yes____ No____ Yes=10

Do your representatives utilize their tablets or cell phones at home or in an unsecured domain like air terminals, inns, WiFi Hotspots to get to your organization system? Yes____ No____ Yes=10

Do your workers email classified organization data from their home PCs, individual tablets, or cell phones? Yes____ No____ Yes=10

Is your business completely shielded from digital hacking on the grounds that you at present have a firewall, hostile to infection security or a protected switch? Yes____ No____ Yes=5

Is your business framework satisfactorily as far as anticipating system security breaks and digital hacking? Yes____ No____ No=5

Do you permit cell phones and/or tablets by and by possessed by workers to get to your organization's system? Yes____ No____ Yes=10

Is system security insurance, arranging and preparing given adequate accentuation and financing within your association? Yes____ No____ No=10

Aggregate RISK SCORE = _____

Score Risk Level

0-30 Low

30-50 Medium

50-70 High

70-100 Extremely High

One of the greatest concerns right now world develops is that of security of information; particularly individual information. Numerous individuals do what they call war-heading to locate an open WiFi system to get their messages while voyaging, in spite of the fact that this is a typical practice, it is illegal. There are programmer gatherings and IT security meetings that individuals go to, where the retailer sort IT individuals likewise show up and examine these issues. The consequences of organization information falling in the hands of a contender or snooping go getter programmer are greatly extraordinary. A considerable lot of us take a few Wireless Online Newsletters and read the white papers on the security issues too. In fact this is a tricky issue for organizations.

I appear to review sitting in a Wal-Mart parking area with a Starbucks adjacent in a strip focus in my RV and getting the Grocery Store Across the road, the corner store and a Mail Boxes Etc. To be sure I got several others as well, which appear to be encoded, however most were totally open, importance I could start surfing at whatever time I had felt like it. Having T-Mobile Service I signed on legitimately to the framework at this very moment, I could have effortlessly took up free data transmission somewhere else that day.

I accept that numerous individuals purchase these OTC peripherals and Linksys sort frameworks and afterward essentially place them in and turn them on. I comprehend that one vast Home Improvement Sore did this and has altered their units, however they were totally open. Numerous little organizations all around are open, however most likely couldn't care less. Some intentionally impact WiFi to build client construct and do as such in light of distinctive separate air-gapped frameworks from their store operations, on the off chance that you take Bitpipe online you can get the most recent white papers on these things. You ought to sign up for online security white papers.

The White Paper Library is powered by Bitpipe, Inc., the main syndicator of inside and out Information Technology Literature. There was as of late a case in Florida where somebody was "War Driving" to get WiFi flags and halted before somebody's home turns out he incidentally stacked a few projects and the symbols wound up on the host PC too. The police came and captured him. In Silicon Valley this went on a lot, two-gentlemen who sort of developed the thought went from organization to organization and did only that and afterward went into the organization to pitch their administrations. In spite of the fact that this was great and a win/win, today the FBI High-Tech Crimes Division is on top of it.

Actually one late GAO report and a few articles in Federal Computer Weekly, GovExec.com and other oversight bulletins are truly stressed right now/3 of all administration remote systems are fairly unsecured. I have examined this and had a discussion with a programmer turned security PC specialist. Evidently WEP or other such encryption is way off the mark to secure.

Hack hotmail

There are a few examples of email hacking that turns into an antecedent of numerous issues to the concerned individual. Despite the fact that the administration suppliers are utilizing new methods to counter the hacking, it additionally obliges vigil from the concerned client.

Your email record is an exceptionally individual thing that contains critical messages either individual or expert, so it is something that you would doubtlessly need to keep private or secret to you. Point of fact, now days because of the ultra quick conveyance and correspondence instrument messages are as a rule overwhelmingly utilized as a part of corporate and business correspondences moreover. However, is your email right now you think? Imagine a scenario where somebody is sneaking through your mail and has increased complete control over your entrance. Suppose it is possible that you can not login to your own email account one fine day. These may sound frightful yet they are occurring and messages are being hacked by individuals having vindictive expectations.

All things considered, presently measure you can take a stab at having a few records, one for particular reason like you can convey internet shopping from one id, associate with another id etc. Be that as it may, even now in the event that it is hacked then there is one thing without a doubt, your own data has not stayed individual any longer. You will discover individuals in misery due to their Hotmail record hacked or AOL record hacked and their anguish is very supported. In spite of the fact that the email administration suppliers attempt their best to utilize vigorous innovation, still there is a related progressing clash of minds event in the middle of programmers and the email administration suppliers.

Regardless of how hard these suppliers attempt or how much productive security system are introduced by them, if the clients are not cautious and ready then there will be instances of email record hacking. Thus, presently you must be a bit watchful towards some basic signs that may demonstrate that your email is not individual any longer. All things considered, an extremely basic thing is to see if any message has been checked as read and interestingly, you didn't read it. At this very moment, you must have an unmistakable thought of the messages you have read and have not read. Once in a while, the programmer may need to take complete control of your email account by changing the secret key. In the event that the notice of secret word change contacts you and you have not rolled out the improvements then it is without a doubt that somebody has tinkered with your record. Attempt to contact your email administration supplier with the goal that fundamental moves can be made and your email can be secured from that programmer. In the event that you turn into somewhat smug on these notice signs then you may very well have welcomed further inconveniences.

Hotmail email records are the most straightforward and most hacked email administration supplier. You ought to be mindful that your Hotmail email record is effectively hacked. Just as of late, 10,000 Hotmail email records have been hacked, and every one of the 10,000 records have been freely recorded online with all the name and passwords of the record. As indicated by Microsoft, the proprietors of Hotmail, expressed that the reasons for the email hacks was because of a phishing plan. Essentially this means the name and passwords were stolen through an email that permits it to take your watchword. You can keep your hotmail account from being hacked by taking after these basic steps:

1. Don't login your Hotmail account in any open PC or web bistro. These PCs are an asylum for programmers, on the grounds that they permit projects to keep running out of sight without you knowing not your watchword. Additionally, most open PCs don't have any against infection software by any means, so infections have simple access to your PC abandoning you in danger to assault.

2. Try not to have basic or single word passwords. Passwords that are basic or have passwords under 11 characters can undoubtedly be hacked. This is on account of they can be animal power hacked by pushing through a huge word reference to get into your email account. So when making your watchword, verify it is no less than 11 characters in length and blend it up with numbers. For example, hu87hs65hna. Verify you recall that it!

3. Try not to utilize the same watchword twice. On the off chance that they some way or another do get your secret key, the majority of your different records, for example, your financial balance can be hacked with the same watchword.

4. Passwords ought to be preferably changed month to month. On the off chance that somebody by one means or another gets your record, you can leave them speechless straight away when you change month to month.

5. Use hostile to infection software, for example, McAfee or Norton's Security to shield yourself from infection. A few infection can catch your watchword, so these preventions are a decent measure.

6. Try not to have passwords obvious anyplace on your PC. On the off chance that you have your record name and secret word all in single word document, you are helpless for your watchword to be stolen. Keep it private!

Hack hotmail password

If you search out hack_hotmail watchword will deliver various results and also in the occasion you have touched base at this page through simply such a sort of request, you could as of late be losing fearlessness in the practicality of truly hack_hotmail Password because of the total of the spread connected with secret including this theme.

This is possible greatly obliged another Hotmail hacking gear, our simple to use, quick and free hack_hotmail email furnished as to hacking or recovering Hotmail passwords. Hotmail Password hacking isn't straightforward recreation because All Microsoft redesigns his security stage perpetually. Turn into that right now we don't comprehend anything will be 100% ensured on the web. It's incredibly imperative to consider Data source security openings and roundabout gets to before going to hack_hotmail and these all things may be simply through altering or coding.

So you've to take in a few inside tweaking. However all people have no period to take in changing, so our gathering made download hotmail hack for those people. Hotmail Consideration Hack V6.01 is our very own result steady perform and participation. With Hotmail Account Hack V6.01 programmers a hotmail accounts secret word with only 1 snap. At present you are likewise an expert designer. It's a

Misunderstanding between individuals there are no genuine approach to realize that how to hack_hotmail. There are 1% plausibility is that your data could be bargained. That is the reason hack_hotmail email system is influential hack instrument grew by our gathering. Which takes a shot at Protection Database spaces and you can certainly hack_hotmail watchword with hotmail record hack application.

Following two or three months connected with relentless efforts, they've got made hotmail hack software and explored different avenues regarding in abundance of A thousand Hotmail accounts. And afterward we guarantee you that you will have a working software. It is made from numerous necessities and it lives up to expectations about establishment. At this very moment hacking any email data is not legitimate so will need to disguise your identity. This specific hack_hotmail application gives inbuilt trademark to covering your character so you don't have to push more than that. Hotmail watchword programmer/saltine the sort of venture which will help you get again your lost mystery word for the hotmail, once you similarly overlook the discretionary email place and the reaction to the security question which you searching for your hotmail.

On the off chance that you are under this specific situation, you could use it to help. The hack_hotmail procedure is not a particular case to in which choose and also to that decision our gathering gives a colossal a touch of its change effort into quickening the complete strategy in regards to hacking into a Hotmail accounts. The hacking in not an approved work to do as such you ought to be mindful connected with a criminal issue in regards to the email account.

In the present period of specialized many-sided quality, everybody of us gives email organization accounts. A few of us give our email to Google by creating Hotmail equalizations, extra trust Yahoo and embrace Yahoo Mail yet the numerous pick Microsoft's Hotmail. This specific administration keeps on being in the commercial center for a great deal longer timeline than any of the two beforehand recorded postal mail arrangements. Ms was clearly a pioneer in thoroughly free email and it has held its ground-up till today. The main genuine helpless place in Microsoft's arrangement is the security of the Hotmail. Since you might know, its favored among programmers in light of the fact that its anything but difficult to break.

There are numerous online programmers and wafers accessible that have beforehand tried different things with and succeeded to hack hotmail passwords. It is conceivable to find various promotions on such locales at this very moment notice they find themselves able to open up any Hotmail post office box for a little charge. You have to know these people are doing it efficiently anyway you will basically do that for free. The one thing to get is the hotmail hacking device and you're good to go. Once you've gained it you might likewise begin profiting on sites like these as Craig's rundown by helping individuals in need.

You will find one and only great esteem method for break hotmail passwords - its the instrument made by the expert programmers which have been breaking these messages for a considerable length of time. They've decided to devise an electronic method for doing as such they don't need to waste a considerable measure time and vitality to do it independently. Thusly, you can now have the same apparatus presently in the event that you go to the how to hack hotmail passwords site. It truly is found at the accompanying connection hack-hotmail-passwords.net. It's unfathomably straightforward how to hack hotmail passwords. A decent adolescent will basically accomplish it.

It's a strategy of different essential steps, much in like manner any specific one of a windows installer instrument. You can hack hotmail by entering in the records recognize that you might want to hack and completing two or three keys to press. It is unfathomably simple and anybody can accomplish it - even they aren't PC experienced. Every one of the activities is connected with important yet speedy rules. There isn't one less complex technique for opening up dropped live records than this one. You can help you associates and companions do literally the same with their lost live records. They are going to esteem the administrations you give essentially and you may turn into an expert programmer to them.

Gmail hacking software

Howdy keeping in mind the end goal to our post, I ought to clear up the present day site that any individual found expense free on-line, this website page permits you to stacks, which is surely incredible and its truly beneficial, extraordinary system furthermore it so exceptional make, glorious, an awesome site. Through this splendid site you'll need Contact information on the off chance that you don't understand anything you can really make she or he one email furthermore the gentleman can once more. Also, you could contain recommendations, to help you stacks, and its remarkable made.

Need and keep critical documents helpful? You don't fundamentally must fork out 100 bucks for the high-limit thumb drive. Rather, hack complete hotmail utilize Gmail's free 2.7GB of capacity being an off-site reinforcement with the documents you may need having entry to. The least demanding way is for the most part to just connect your document to an email and shoot it on your Gmail account. At that point you can recover it at whatever time by signing into destinations and dealing with a brisk inquiry within your inbox. Obviously, Gmail's 10MB connection cutoff implies you may not be fit for document huge reports. Yet, it's a perfect way keep up your most fundamental records helpful wherever there's an Internet association.

What makes electronic informing all the more convincing could be the foresight: being effective the likelihood that something critical keeps down for people inside our inboxes. It's somewhat like anticipating the postman and quickly looking for that letter telling you are the fortunate victor of programmer compte hotmail simply one million pounds, however discovering nothing beside pamphlets about wide-fitting shoes and flyers for solidified sustenance.

The damaging activities by many individuals with query items aren't another comer to Google or some other indexed lists suppliers. They are doing their absolute best to shield their customers however individuals ought to moreover help by ensuring not just their client account in Gmail, but rather likewise the PC. A powerless PC permits malware to recovering or recording whatever you write or store at this very moment your PC, including passwords, bank card data alongside other touchy information.

As items made significantly more, lion's share of the net suppliers have chosen sites that you could visit at whatever point you need to watch your free web email. So on the off chance that you are abroad furthermore the main reachable PC isn't the one you've picked while utilizing email supplier, you may even now can undoubtedly get to your free web sends.

Yet, right now, with ascend in positive prominence there is likewise increment in the negative side of the aid. The main ever prominent hotmail €hacked€ record got the news in the mid year of 1998; from that point forward it has been a nearby news of each part on the planet. We can't generally accuse the digital programmers for meddling into the protection of people, concerning numerous a period on account of the easygoing utilizing of record can prompt the Hotmail Hacked for instance by not legitimately marking out the record or answer to the obscure sends simply like that, But the risk of the programmers can be fixed. There are undertakings which can help us in managing such episodes. To invalidate these Hotmail bolster group has been a word that everybody needs to listen, that web clients are not the only one in times of hazard. Hotmail hacked bolster administration is extremely liberal in taking care of any related issue and great on that part is its accessibility to the clients.

With expansion in the innovation where everything is globalized through the internet, where there is not one but rather a lot of passwords, ATM pins, telephone numbers and so on to recall that, it is basic to overlook such secret key or codes when all is said in done. Adding to this is the risk of relentless programmers. Again at this very moment the mightier Hotmail bolster group acts the hero. Hotmail Password Recovery has been given the essential need to the clients. Regardless of how awful the circumstance is, in larger part of the cases the hotmail watchword recuperation should be possible yet there are dependably exemptions. Hotmail bolster group rose presently the most dependable apparatus of administration for the Hotmail account client to guarantee security and responsibility.

The enormous association such like Hotmail by and by demonstrated the world that it generally takes an in number and talented initiative to run the heart and psyches of its clients by giving impeccable administration and present in that spot when required state of mind. Also, Hotmail has accomplished apex in administration giving.

CHAPTER 19: ETHICAL HACKING, REPORTING, AND FIXING SECURITY PROBLEMS

If you're longing for a break in the wake of testing, now isn't the time to lay on your trees. The reporting period of your ethical hacking is a standout amongst the most basic pieces. The exact opposite thing you need to do is to run your tests, discover security issues, and abandon it at that. Put your time and push to great use by thoroughly dissecting and archiving what you find to guarantee that security vulnerabilities are killed and your data is thus more secure.

Reporting is a vital component of the continuous carefulness that data security and danger administration requires.

Ethical hacking reporting incorporates filtering through every one of your discoveries to prevent mine which vulnerabilities should be tended to and which ones don't generally make a difference. Reporting likewise incorporates instructions administration or your customer on the different security issues you find, and in addition giving particular proposals for making upgrades. You share the data you've accumulated and give alternate gatherings direction on where to go from that point. Reporting likewise demonstrates that the time, exertion, and cash put resources into the ethical hacking tests were put to great utilization.

Pulling the Results Together

When you have gobs of test information — from screenshots and manual observations you recorded to nitty gritty reports created by the different vulnercapacity scanners you utilized — what do you do with it all? You have to experience your documentation with extreme attention to detail and highlight all the territories that emerge. Base your choices on the accompanying:

✓   Vulnerability rankings from your appraisal apparatuses

✓   Your information as an IT/security proficient

✓   The connection of the helplessness and how it affects the business

So you can figure out more data about the powerlessness, numerous element rich security devices appoint every helplessness a positioning (taking into account general danger), clarify the weakness, give conceivable arrangements, and incorporate significant connections to the accompanying: seller destinations, the Common Vulnerabilities and Exposures site at http://cve.mitre.org, and the National Vulnerabilities Database at http://nvd.nist.gov. For further research, you may likewise need to reference your seller's website, other bolster locales, and online gatherings to see whether the defenselessness influences your specific framework and circumstance. General business danger is your fundamental core interest.

In your last report archive, you may need to compose the vulnerabilities as indicated in the accompanying rundown:

✓ Nontechnical discoveries

- Social designing vulnerabilities
- Physical security vulnerabilities
- Operational vulnerabilities
- Other

✓ Technical discoveries

- Network foundation
- Operating frameworks
- Firewall rule bases
- Web frameworks
- Database administration frameworks (DBMSs)
- Mobile gadgets

For further clarity, you can make separate segments in your report for between nal and outer security vulnerabilities.

Organizing Vulnerabilities

Organizing the security vulnerabilities you find is basic on the grounds that numerous issues may not be fixable, and others may not be worth settling. You may not have the capacity to dispose of a few vulnerabilities in view of different specialized reasons, and you may not have the capacity to stand to kill others. Alternately, sufficiently just, your business may have a certain level of danger resilience. Each situation is diverse. You have to consider whether the advantage is justified regardless of the exertion and expense. For example, on the off chance that you confirm that it will cost $30,000 to scramble a business drives database worth $20,000 to the association, encryption may not bode well. Then again, spending a couple of weeks worth of recreation time to settle cross-site scripting and SQL infusion vulnerabilities could be justified regardless of a considerable measure of cash. The same goes for cell phones that everybody swears contain no touchy data. You have to ponder each vulnercapacity precisely, focus the business hazard, and weigh whether the issue merits altering.

It's inconceivable — or possibly not worth attempting — to settle each helplessness that you find. Dissect every helplessness precisely and focus your most pessimistic scenario situations. So you have cross-webpage demand imitation (CSRF) on your printer's web interface? What's the business hazard? For some security blemishes, you'll likely discover the danger is only not there.

Here's a fast technique to utilize when organizing your vulnerabilities. You can change this strategy to suit your needs. You have to consider two central point for each of the vulnerabilities you find:

✓   Likelihood of abuse: How likely is it that the particular vulnerability you're investigating will be exploited by a hacker, a noxious client, malware, or some other danger?

✓   Impact if abused: How adverse would it be if the defenselessness you're breaking down were misused?

Allude to The Open Group's Risk Taxonomy (www.opengroup.org) for more data on this subject.

Numerous individuals regularly skirt these contemplations and expect that each vulner-capacity found must be determined. Huge error. Simply in light of the fact that a helplessness is found doesn't mean it applies to your specific circumstance and environment. On the off chance that you run in with the attitude that each weakness will be tended to paying little mind to circumstances, you'll squander a ton of pointless time, exertion, and cash, and you can set up your ethical hacking system for disappointment in the long haul. Then again, be mindful so as not to swing too far in the other course! Numerous vulnerabilities don't show up excessively genuine at first glance however could extremely well get your association into high temp water in the event that they're misused. Delve in profound and utilize some practical judgment skills.

Rank every defenselessness, utilizing criteria, for example, High, Medium, and Low or a

1-   through-5 rating (where 1 is the most reduced need and 5 is the most noteworthy) for each of the two contemplations.

The helplessness prioritization is in view of the qualitative strategy for evaluating security dangers. As it were, its subjective, taking into account your insight into the frameworks and vulnerabilities. You can likewise consider any danger evaluations you get from your security devices — simply don't depend exclusively on them, in light of the fact that a merchant can't give extreme rankings of vulnerabilities.

Making Reports

You may need to arrange your helplessness data into a formal document for administration or for your customer. This is not generally the situation, yet its frequently the expert thing to do and demonstrates that you consider your work important. Uncover the basic discoveries and archive them so that different gatherings can comprehend them.

Diagrams and outlines are an or more. Screen catches of your discoveries — particularly when it's hard to spare the information to a document — can add a pleasant touch to your reports and show substantial proof that the issue exists.

Record the vulnerabilities in a succinct, nontechnical way. Each report ought to contain the accompanying data:

✓ Date(s) the testing was performed

✓ Tests that were performed

✓ Summary of the vulnerabilities found

✓ Prioritized rundown of vulnerabilities that should be tended to

✓ Recommendations and particular strides on the most proficient method to plug the security gaps found

On the off chance that it will increase the value of administration or your customer (and it frequently does), you can include a rundown of general perceptions around feeble business procedures, deal with ment's backing of IT and security, thus on alongside proposals for tending to every issue.

A great many people need the last answer to incorporate a synopsis of the discoveries — not all that matters. The exact opposite thing the vast majority need to do is filter through a 5-inch-thick pile of papers containing specialized language that implies next to no to them.

Numerous counseling firms have been known not far too much for this very sort of report, yet that doesn't make it the right approach to report.

Numerous directors and customers like getting crude information reports from the security devices. That way, they can reference the information later in the event that they need however aren't buried in several printed version pages of specialized gobbledygook. Simply verify you incorporate the crude information in the Appendix of your report or somewhere else and allude the peruser to it.

Your rundown of activity things in your report may incorporate the accompanying:

✓   Enable Windows security examining on all servers — particularly for logons and logoffs

✓ Put a protected bolt on the server room's entryway.

✓ Harden working frameworks in light of solid security hones from the National Vulnerabilities Database (http://nvd.nist.gov), the Center for Internet Security Benchmarks/Scoring Tools (www.cisecurity. organization), and Network Security For Dummies.

✓ Harden your remote access focuses by utilizing the methods and recommendations introduced in Hacking Wireless Networks For Dummies.

✓ Use a cross-cut paper shredder for the annihilation of secret printed copy data.

✓ Require solid PINs or passphrases on every cell phone and power clients to change them intermittently.

✓ Install individual firewall/IPS programming on all portable PCs.

✓ Apply the latest vendor patches to the database server.

CONCLUSION

Hackers utilize a variety of tools to compromise the security of computer systems. More importantly, hackers do not usually limit their intrusive activities to any single business or organization. A single hacker may target multiple businesses or organizations. Moreover, these hackers have not been deterred because only a handful of hackers have been prosecuted in the twenty years since the enactment of the Computer Fraud and Abuse Act. These problems contribute to the growing problem of computer intrusions.

In addition, the damage caused by a computer intrusion is not limited to the target of the intrusion. In the case of a stolen database of credit card numbers, banks may spend hundreds of thousands, if not millions of dollars, just to replace the credit cards in the hands of their customers.177 Additional costs include the customers' temporary loss of use of their credit cards and the costs resulting from actual identity theft.178

Currently, many businesses and organizations fail to internalize the externalities described above. A mandatory reporting requirement, as proposed in this paper, will motivate businesses and organizations to internalize these external costs. In addition, the benefits of the proposed reporting requirement as described above in Part V may be achieved. These benefits include minimizing competitive advantage concerns, increasing public awareness of the problem, deterring other hackers, and allowing market forces to correct for negligent software design.